# Perfectly Ordinary

## Buddhist Teachings for Everyday Life

By Alex Kakuyo

This book reflects the author's present recollections of experiences over time. Some names and characteristics have been changed, some events have been compressed, and some dialogue has been recreated.

The essays herein are not intended for medical treatment, psychological, or psychiatric therapy. If you have a medical condition or concern, please consult a licensed health care professional.

First e-book edition March 2020

Independently Published

www.thesameoldzen.com

Please send inquiries to sameoldzen@gmail.com

# Table of Contents

# INTRODUCTION

A young boy was sitting on a park bench when a Buddhist minister from the local temple sat down next to him. They made small talk for a while, and then the youth started asking questions related to Buddhist practice.

"Teacher," he asked, "what is the Buddhist Pureland?"

The minister smiled, as this was his third favorite thing to discuss. Then he said, "The Buddhist Pureland is the perfect place for us to practice the Dharma. When we go there, we find everything we need to realize enlightenment." The boy nodded when he heard this. But it wasn't long before he thought of another question.

"Teacher," he asked, "where is the Pureland located?"

Upon hearing this, the minister smiled even wider because this was his second favorite thing to discuss. "Well," he said, "no one knows the exact location. But the sutras tell us that the Buddhist Pureland, which has the perfect conditions for us to realize enlightenment, is in the west."

The young boy thought about this for a moment, and for a while, a look of contentment appeared on his face. But as time passed, his look of contentment changed to one of confusion, and the teacher could tell that he was thinking hard about something.

Finally, the boy said, "teacher, in school, we learned that the earth is round. So, if I keep going west to find the

Buddhist Pureland, which is the perfect place to realize enlightenment, I'll end up back where I started."

Upon hearing this, the Buddhist minister laughed with joy because this was his first favorite thing to discuss. Then he turned to the young boy, looked deeply into his eyes, and said, "Exactly!"

This story was told to me by Reverend Koyo Kubose, president of the Bright Dawn Center of Oneness Buddhism. I enjoy retelling it because it perfectly sums up my approach to Buddhist practice. Human history is filled with people going on dangerous quests in search of inner peace. Whether it's the holy grail, the fountain of youth, or the Buddhist Pureland, we always think that what we're looking for lies just over the horizon.

For many years, I, too, thought that I had to venture off somewhere else to find wholeness and inner peace. For a while, I felt that money and adventure would provide what I was looking for, so I enlisted in the Marines, and after that, I pursued a career in corporate America. I learned many great and useful things from these experiences, but they still left me with an itch that I couldn't scratch. So, I decided that enlightenment was the answer. I started practicing Buddhism, and after several years of practice I quit my job, gave away most of my worldly possessions, and I spent eight months meditating and working on organic farms to find it.

But like the young boy in the story, it wasn't long before I realized that inner peace can't be found outside of ourselves. And the perfect place to realize enlightenment is exactly where we are. So, I've laid out this book in a precise way. I discuss the core teachings of Buddhism in the Four Noble Truths and the Noble Eightfold Path along with the ordinary life events that taught me how to embody those teachings in daily life.

I adapted some of these essays from articles that appear on my blog, *The Same Old Zen*. Others came from talks that I've delivered in my role as a Buddhist teacher. And still others are entirely original to this text, so I'm confident that everyone who reads this will find something interesting to chew on.

This book isn't a memoir. However, I spend a lot of time speaking from personal experience. And while I've done my best to tell the stories accurately, it's inevitable that my recollection of events may differ from other people. Also, in some places, names and location details have been changed to respect the privacy of the people involved.

However, I've done my best to ensure that any changes will not detract from my final goal, which is to communicate how everyday experiences can help us find Buddha in everyday life and stop our endless wanting for something more.

# The Four Noble Truths

The Four Noble Truths represent the capstone of Buddhist practice. They provide a clear explanation of the nature of reality along with an ethical framework that helps us live skillfully and be of benefit to ourselves and others.

However, it can be challenging to decipher the subtleties of each truth and how to implement them in daily life. The key things that need to be understood are as follows:

## 1. LIFE IS SUFFERING

We need to unpack this a bit because it can be disconcerting if taken at face value. The word "suffering" has a different meaning in Buddhism than it does in Western culture. The death of a loved one or the loss of a job qualifies as suffering. However, a child who forgets to take out the trash is also a source of pain.

So, suffering is not a finite thing. Instead, it's a spectrum of experiences that we deem to be unpleasant or painful. The Buddha stated, "Life is suffering" because he grouped all our experiences into one of three categories:

1. Things we want but can't have (e.g., $1 million)
2. Things we have but don't want (e.g., a broken ankle)
3. Things we have, and enjoy, but lose due to the transient nature of life (e.g., our youth or a close friendship)

In this way, it's easy to see that everything we desire causes us suffering either in the short term for items in groups 1 and 2 or in the long term for items in group 3.

Another way to look at the teaching is to use a more literal translation of the original Pali. The Pali word for suffering is "dukkha," which can also be taken to mean "hard to carry" or "difficult to bear."[1] So, another way to read the First Noble Truth is "Life is difficult to bear." Of course, that begs the question "What makes life so difficult?"

## 2. SUFFERING IS CAUSED BY DESIRE

The Second Noble Truth refers to the three types of suffering that we referenced earlier. An easy way to think about it is to imagine we're carrying a backpack, and it's filled with stones. Each stone represents something we desire, and the more attached we become to that desire, the larger the stone becomes. So, the greater our desire grows, the heavier our packs become, which results in our lives being more difficult to bear.

In contrast, the smaller our desire becomes, the lighter our packs become, and the easier our lives are to bear. One might argue that desire is a natural part of life, and they'd be correct. That's why the first noble truth reminds us that suffering is also a natural part of life. Our desire and our suffering feed each other in a never-ending cycle. Thankfully, all is not lost. If the first noble truth tells us our problem and the second tells us the cause, then the third noble truth tells us the solution for escaping this endless cycle of suffering.

## 3. THE WAY TO END SUFFERING IS TO END DESIRE

This one is straightforward. If our lives are difficult to bear because we're carrying too many stones/desires around, then the obvious solution is to get rid of the stones! Buddha took this idea about as far one could reasonably go, stripping his life of everything except the essentials of food, clothing, medicine, and shelter.

Since these items are necessary for life, he trained himself and his monastics to use them skillfully as opposed to renouncing them completely. For example, they only ate food that lay people donated to them, and they were only allowed to beg for food before noon.

This practice allowed them to meet their nutritional needs without feeding into any desires or aversions toward specific foods. It also kept them from becoming a burden on the lay people who supported them. However, they also worked to limit their desires by limiting their personal possessions.

The monks' only possessions were two sets of robes and a begging bowl. They didn't have families or permanent living quarters because they wanted as few stones/desires in their backpacks as possible. The general attitude could best be described as "I'm going to lose it anyway, so why not let go of it all now."

This is a reasonable attitude for a monastic to take. However, it doesn't translate well for people who have jobs, families, student loans, etc. But the teaching is still useful if we approach it differently. As lay people, we can use our inner wisdom to examine each desire that we are carrying around and decide if we can safely discard it. If so, then getting rid of it will inevitably lighten our packs, and ease our suffering.

However, if we can't discard it, we must learn how to work skillfully with that desire and make ourselves more spiritually resilient to carry it. The fourth noble truth explains how to do this.

## 4. The Way to End Desire is the Noble Eightfold Path

The Eightfold path is a set of tenets that were laid out by Buddha to help us live skillfully in a non-harming way. It provides benchmarks for measuring our adherence to the Buddhist path along with techniques for quieting the anxious mind.

The tenets of the Eightfold path are as follows:

**Right View** - We must work to see the world as it truly is - free from our preference of how it should be.

**Right Intention** - We must be committed to morality and ethical behavior in our dealings with others.

**Right Speech** - We must abstain from speech that is either untrue or divisive and use words that improve the lives of ourselves and others.

**Right Action** - We must abstain from causing harm to ourselves and other sentient beings

**Right Livelihood -** We must earn a living in a way that doesn't cause damage to ourselves or other sentient beings - abstaining from the slave trade, weapon sales, animal butchery, and the sale of intoxicants and poisons.

**Right Effort -** We must abstain from giving in to unwholesome mind-states (e.g., greed, anger, and ignorance) while simultaneously working to arouse wholesome mind-states (e.g., gratitude, faith, and compassion).

**Right Mindfulness -** We must learn about the nature of reality by contemplating our minds, bodies, feelings, and mental objects.

**Right Concentration -** We must practice meditation daily to free ourselves from negative mental impulses.

Learning to embody each of the eight tenets and adhere to their guidelines is a lifelong practice, which results in the cessation of suffering in our daily lives. As we do this, we become bored with our desires and learn to live lives of gratitude and faith. Eventually, the teachings become a part of us, and we don't even have to think about them. Instead, we embody and manifest them in each moment as we move through the world.

# Life Is Suffering

# Suffering and Snow Days

The first noble truth of Buddhism states, "Life is suffering." This can be off-putting for some people as it seems to suggest that there is no joy to be found in human existence. However, this couldn't be further from the truth. The first noble truth doesn't deny the fun parts of life (family, nature, good health, etc.). Instead, it reminds us that those things occur in the midst of all the unpleasant parts (death, sickness, bad relationships, etc.). And we can't have one without the other.

For example, imagine that we wake up one morning and the weatherman tells us that it's cold outside with three feet of snow on the ground. If we react to his pronouncement with fear and choose to never leave the house, then our lives will be very gray and shallow. On the other hand, if we want to ignore the weatherman's prediction, venturing outside in shorts and flip flops, then we'll suffer a great deal as the snow freezes our skin.

But if we accept the inherently cold nature of snow, then we can prepare for it by wearing a heavy coat, boots, and gloves when we go outside. If we do this, the weather conditions won't bother us as much, and we may even have some fun! Our warm clothing will allow us to build snowmen, have snowball fights, and maybe also go sledding with our friends! But none of this is possible if we don't prepare correctly.

Similarly, when Buddha says, "Life is suffering," he uses the same tone of voice as someone who says, "It's cold outside." It isn't a proclamation designed to make us fearful. Instead, it's meant to be a healthy reminder that suffering exists in the world, and we need to prepare.

Of course, we don't have to listen. Instead, we can respond to the world by attempting to hide from it, refusing to do anything that might be challenging or unpleasant. But this results in a life free from vigor and accomplishment. Similarly, we can try and distract ourselves, filling our mind with a steady stream of sensual pleasure and social media. But this only works for a short time. Inevitably, life will catch up with us, and it will bring our pain with it.

We can't remove suffering from life any more than we can remove snow from a snowman. With this in mind, we prepare for the snow because we enjoy building snowmen. And we prepare for suffering because we enjoy living life. For a Buddhist, wisdom is our heavy coat. Morality is our heavy boots. And meditation is the pair of gloves that prepares us for living in a cold, snow-covered world.

And as our practice gets stronger, our suffering becomes less. Until the day comes when we don't see the snow; we just see the snowmen. We don't worry about the cold; we just enjoy our hot chocolate. And we don't fear life's suffering because we're ready to deal with it.

**Lesson:** Don't be afraid of suffering. Make a snowman out of it.

## A Single Act of Kindness

When I was 11 years old, I attended a Toys for Tots charity event with my Cub Scout troop. Toys for Tots is an annual charity event run by the U.S. Marines that collects toys for disadvantaged children and delivers them to families, ensuring that each kid gets at least a few toys for Christmas.

My scout troop had spent the last few months collecting toys, and we were having a party at the local VFW where the kids and parents could chat, honor any scouts who'd recently earned new merit badges, and deliver the toys to the Marines for distribution. Traditionally, the night would end with a "surprise" uniform inspection from a visiting Marine and a recitation of the scout oath.

My knowledge of the military was limited to what I'd seen in G.I. Joe cartoons on TV, but I knew enough to know that the Marines were a big deal. I also knew that part of military discipline was being able to stand at attention without moving.

So, when the adults put us in lines for the inspection, I decided that I was going to show everyone what I could do. While the other scouts stood around laughing and joking around, I stood at attention and did my best to be stone still.

I watched the Marine sergeant out of the corner of my eye as he walked up and down the rows chatting with each scout and encouraging them to work hard on their merit badges. When he finally got to me, he smiled and asked me my name. But I didn't respond. I knew you weren't supposed to talk at the position of attention, and I thought he was testing me.

He looked confused for a moment until one of the grown-ups hurried over and explained what I was doing. At that point, he smiled again and said, "at ease."

I smiled back, placed my hands in the small of my back, and spread my feet to shoulders width apart. Now we could talk. We chatted for several minutes. I told him about the merit badges I was working on and the toy truck that I'd bought with my allowance to donate. Then he asked me if there were any Marines in my family, and I told him no. He nodded thoughtfully before bending over and looking me square in the eyes. "Well," he said quietly, "I think you have what it takes to be the first one."

It felt like I grew three feet taller at that moment. Then he stood up straight, called me back to attention, and walked away to speak with another scout.

Over the years, I've thought a lot about why that moment meant so much to me. From what I can tell, it had less to do with what was said and more to do with what was going on in other parts of my life. I was a small, socially awkward kid who didn't have many friends. I was having a difficult time at school, and my self-confidence wasn't very high.

Amid all that, a Marine took the time to look me in the eye and tell me that I was special. He made me feel seen and appreciated at a time when I mostly felt invisible. In the sea of suffering that was my life at 11 years old, his act of kindness was a life jacket.

Of course, he couldn't have known that. He couldn't have known that our conversation would shift the entire trajectory of my life, resulting in my taking the oath of enlistment several years later and becoming a U.S. Marine myself. He just saw an opportunity to be kind, and he took it. The rest took care of itself.

That's important because the amount of suffering in the world can be overwhelming. In the face of endless wars and natural disasters one might wonder if it's worth trying to fix it.

But when I start to have these thoughts, I think back to that night at the Toys for Tots event. I think back to the five-minute conversation that changed my life forever. And I remember that we don't have to do something about every bit of suffering in the world. We only need to deal with what's in front of us.

A single act of kindness - a smile, a compliment, a helping hand can be the catalyst for years of generosity and goodwill. One good deed can change an entire life for the better. We don't need to save the whole world from suffering. We need to pay attention and look for chances to be kind in this present moment. If we do that, the rest will take care of itself.

**Lesson:** Don't save the world from suffering. Just save the person in front of you.

## Building Mt. Suribachi

At the age of 19, I enlisted in the United States Marine Corps Reserves. At that point, I had a year of college under my belt, and I enjoyed academia. But there was a part of me that wanted something more, that knew that there was more to life than going to parties and studying for exams.

Some of my favorite authors like Pat Conroy and Ernest Hemingway had military experience. And I wanted to be like them. I wanted to live through the things that I'd read about as a kid. I wanted to be pushed to my breaking point. I wanted to do something hard.

So, when I got home for summer break, I walked into the recruiter's office, signed some paperwork, and jumped on a plane for Parris Island, South Carolina, a few weeks later. Based on the online research that I did before arriving at recruit training I thought I was well-prepared for what I was about to experience.

I'd done my best to learn basic military knowledge, and I was physically fit due to endless hours spent weight training in my college's gym. I honestly thought that I could breeze through the training. I was dead wrong.

Everyone struggles with something when they cycle through Parris Island. After all, the training is designed to break you. Some people get there and find out they can't run the three miles required to pass the Marine Corps physical fitness test. Other can't march or shoot accurately on the rifle range. For me, the challenge was a mental one.

As a freshman in college, I had only just started to get used to the freedoms and responsibilities that come with being an adult. I was paying bills, choosing classes, and making friends all on my own. To be sure, I didn't have it all figured out, but it felt great to be independent.

The Marine Corps took those feelings and crushed them. Suddenly, I couldn't pick what clothes I wanted to wear or what food I wanted to eat. I couldn't even use the restroom without a drill instructor's permission.

In the past, I'd always been able to game the system or change my circumstances when life was hard. But that wasn't an option in recruit training. The standards were non-negotiable, the rules were iron-clad, and I only had two choices. Get with the program and become a Marine or quit and go home in disgrace.

What made it worse was that the drill instructors would play different types of mind games with the recruits. For example, one standard game was called "Mt. Suribachi." It involved 70 recruits being forced to dump out the contents of their footlockers in the middle of the squad bay to build a makeshift "Mt. Suribachi."

Then the drill instructor would countdown from 30, and recruits were expected to get all of their gear out of the giant pile of stuff, put it back in the footlockers, and be standing in front of their rack at the position of attention before the drill instructor got to zero. If a single recruit didn't make it in time, the whole platoon had to empty their footlockers and start again.

It sounds sadistic, but it was an essential part of the training. The Marine Corps needed to know that we could operate under high levels of stress. Games like Mt. Suribachi were one way to ensure that we wouldn't crack under pressure.

Unfortunately, I didn't adapt well to this part of the training. I didn't like getting punished for my own mistakes much less the errors of other people. On top of that, there was no rhyme or reason to it. Sometimes, games were a form of punishment; sometimes they were done "just because."

This all resulted in a lot of mental suffering on my part. I was angry at myself for enlisting, I was mad at the drill instructors for being cruel, and I was shocked by the sudden turn that my life had taken.

The breaking point came one day when a fellow recruit forgot to lock his footlocker. This was a cardinal offense as security is a top priority in the military. The drill instructor who caught him decided that not only would he be punished, but the recruits standing to his left and right would suffer as well. He was at fault for not securing his gear, but we were also at fault for not reminding him to do it.

As a result, the three of us were ordered to run out of the squad bay and go down to "the pit." The pit was a giant sandbox that drill instructors used to punish recruits by making them do calisthenics in the hot sand. Over time, the sand would get stuck to our skin and work its way into our underwear. It was quite unpleasant.

As we rolled around in the sand doing crunches, pushups, and mountain-climbers, my mind was racing. At this point, I had another seven weeks left before I graduated. It seemed like an eternity, and for the 357$^{th}$ time that day I thought about quitting.

I even started to rationalize it in my head and think about what I would tell my family. But before I could get very far with my plans, the drill instructor screamed, "Attention!"

"Attention, aye sir," I screamed in unison with my fellow recruits.

"Get your gear on, go back to the squad bay, and prepare for chow," he screamed.

"Prepare for chow, aye sir," we responded.

"Ready," he yelled.

"Discipline," we responded.

"Move," he growled.

Upon hearing the command, we screamed at the top of our lungs, and then took off running for the squad bay with him bringing up the rear. As we ran, the drill instructor yelled at us to move faster, but I could barely hear him. The wheels in my head were turning more quickly than before. We'd only been in the pit for a couple of minutes. "Why was he going so easy on us," I wondered. And then it hit me. We had to go to chow.

As I put two and two together, I realized that the recruits were on a strict schedule each day, but so were the drill instructors. They had to get us to the chow hall for breakfast, lunch, and dinner at the same time each day. And they had to get us in our racks for lights out at the same time each night.

They could torture us in-between those times. But they couldn't stop the clock. No matter what happened, sooner or later they'd have to take us to the chow hall.

There was no way that I could deal with seven more weeks of going to the pit and throwing my stuff all over the squad bay. But I could suck it up for a few hours until my next meal. And if I did that enough times, I'd make it to graduation.

As I look at this experience through a Buddhist lens, I realize that the strategy I used for coping with discomfort as a Marine recruit also works for life in general. Recruit training contains suffering so that young men can become Marines. And life contains suffering so that we can realize enlightenment.

If there were no discomfort in life, we'd have no opportunities to practice Buddhism. But there's lots of suffering in life, so we all have many opportunities to realize enlightenment. However, suffering can be difficult to bear. And during times when it's especially challenging, it's helpful to remind ourselves that nothing lasts forever.

Buddhism provides many tools to help us skillfully work with pain. But when all else fails, we can remind ourselves that even if things seem bad now, there's always a time limit to suffering.

**Lesson:** Be patient, things will get better

# Accepting Life's Boulders

According to Greek mythology, Sisyphus was a king in modern-day Corinth and a renowned trickster of both men and gods alike. He famously escaped death by convincing Hades, the god of the underworld, to put on a set of handcuffs to show him how they worked. Once Hades was locked up, Sisyphus threw him in a closet and continued living his life as if nothing had happened.

Despite his cunning, however, Sisyphus did eventually die, and his soul went to Tartarus, the ancient Greek version of hell. As punishment for his crimes, he was condemned to spend eternity rolling a massive boulder up a hill each day only to have it roll down again once it got to the top.

It was a grueling task. Between the boredom of doing the same thing every day and the back-breaking labor of pushing a boulder, I imagine that Sisyphus endured great suffering. In this way, his story is an excellent metaphor for our lives.

We all have boulders/suffering that we deal with every day. Perhaps it's a job we hate. Maybe it's poor finances or a body that doesn't work the way it should. Sometimes, we can change our circumstances and alleviate discomfort. But sometimes we can't. Sometimes we're like Sisyphus, left with no other choice than to roll a giant rock uphill each day.

In our weaker moments, we try to hide from our pain. We close our eyes and pretend it doesn't exist. We numb ourselves with television, lousy food, social media, etc. in the hopes that we can find an escape. But these are temporary solutions that leave us feeling unsatisfied. Despite our best efforts, the boulder is always there.

Other times, we grit our teeth and suffer violently. We rage against the boulder as we push it up the hill. We curse as waves of grief and frustration wash over us with each step. And when we finally reach the summit only to have the rock slip from our fingers, we stand there for a moment. And we wonder why life is so hard.

In contrast, when a student asked Rev. Gyomay Kubose about suffering, he stated: "Acceptance is transcendence." It sounds strange, but this is the Buddhist view on dealing with mental anguish. We don't try to escape it, and we don't get bent out of shape about it.

Instead, we take responsibility for our pain. We put it under a microscope, and we study it. We tear it apart until we find the root cause of our anguish (hurt feelings, disappointment, fear, etc.), and then we learn to be at peace with those feelings.

Once we accept the boulders in our life, a shift occurs in our thinking. Our pain lessens as we stop piling emotional baggage on top of it. Eventually, the job sucks, but we tolerate it. Finances are tight, but we make it work. And our life gets a little better because we've trained our mind to stop making it worse. Over time, we may even learn to appreciate the experience, unpleasant though it may be, and laugh a little at our plight. After all, life can only be what it is. And it's funny each time we think it can/should be different.

Finally, we begin to enjoy life not in spite of our suffering but because of it. Because this pain, this struggle, this constant fight is the juice of life. It's how we know we're alive. Thus, we end our suffering not by trying to escape it but by learning to embrace it.

**Lesson:** If we accept our suffering, we can learn to enjoy it.

## Oryoki Disaster

Oryoki is a Japanese word that roughly translates to "just enough." In Buddhist circles, it's used in the context of oryoki bowl sets that students use during meditation retreats. The bowls come in a set of four with each one stacking inside of the others, complete with chopsticks, a metal spoon, and a handkerchief that wraps around the entire dish set.

During an oryoki-style meal, practitioners eat in a ritualized way. Everything from how we wash the bowls to where the spoon is placed at the end of a meal is tightly controlled. The ritual reminds each student that they should never take meals for granted. After all, many sentient beings worked in concert to grow, cultivate, and transport that food to the temple for their benefit.

So, by paying close attention when we eat, we express gratitude for the nourishment we receive. Additionally, it serves as an exercise in mindfulness as we take what we need from the world without creating unnecessary trouble for others. We take "just enough" food, eat in silence, and wash our bowls thoroughly when we're finished. The result is that by the end of the meal a casual observer would think nothing had transpired.

My first experience with an oryoki-style meal came during a retreat at the Indianapolis Zen Center. We'd spent the morning doing the customary 108 bows to cleanse our defilements, chanting, and practicing seated meditation. The center was kind enough to provide us with oryoki bowls to eat from, so I and the other students each grabbed our utensils at the appointed time and sat down on our cushions.

When JDPSN (*Ji Do Poep Sa Nim*) Linc Rhodes, the abbot of Indianapolis Zen Center, gave the signal we all opened our oryoki sets and laid out the bowls in a 2x2 square. Each person used their handkerchief as a makeshift tablecloth to ensure no crumbs would fall on the hardwood floor.

Next, the senior students came around with trays of food, which held brown rice, fruit, and a variety of cooked vegetables. Each person waited with their palms together in gassho until the server was standing in front of them. Then they took some food for themselves, being careful to leave enough for everyone else, and then sat with their hands in gassho. No one could begin eating until everyone had food.

When the meal was over, another student came around with hot tea and poured it into one of our bowls. Using our fingers and chopsticks, we used the tea to clean each bowl individually until we had a cold tea/ food mixture in the final dish. When the retreat leader gave the signal, each student drank the brew and left a small amount of liquid that would be used later as an offering for the hungry ghosts.

That's where the trouble started. I'd been nursing a minor back strain for a week leading up to the retreat, and during the meal, it began to bother me with tiny spasms running up and down my left side. When it came time for me to pour out my offering to the hungry ghosts, I had a particularly bad spasm that resulted in me spilling my water and half-eaten food on the woman seated next to me.

I started to utter an apology, and then I remembered that I wasn't supposed to talk. In the end, I let out a weird screech that sounded like a cross between a squeaky door and a dying parrot.

Unsure of what to do, I glanced around the room, but no one moved or looked in my direction. When I turned my gaze back to the woman sitting next to me, she was gone. She returned a few moments later with a handful of paper towels and quickly cleaned up the mess around her cushion.

Then she stood up and left the meditation hall (I assume to throw the paper towels away) before returning to her cushion. Without saying a word, she placed her hands in gassho and stared at the ground in front of her. The entire sequence probably took about two minutes, but it was an eternity in my mind.

"Ahem," the woman gently cleared her throat and looked pointedly at the oryoki bowl that I was holding out of the corner of her eye. Then she looked up the senior student who was waiting patiently in front of me with the offering bowl. I still had a tiny bit of liquid left after the spill, so I poured it into the offering bowl and bowed.

Suffering comes at us in a variety of ways throughout our lives. Sometimes, it's in the form of a sick loved one or a traffic jam when we're running late for work. Other times, it's a bowl of water being spilled on us when we're sitting quietly during a retreat. But while it can take many forms, the first noble truth assures us that we will experience suffering.

If we're unprepared for this, if we think that bad things shouldn't happen, then this can result in feelings of sadness, anger, and bitterness. But if we're able to accept our suffering as a natural part of life, like that wise woman did when I spilled water on her, then we're able to react skillfully in the moment.

She had every right to be angry at the newbie who clumsily made a mess on her cushion. But she didn't do that. Instead, while I was feeling sorry for myself, she got up, solved the problem, and returned to her seat like a pro.

Her actions were a perfect embodiment of Buddhist practice in daily life. We start each day on our cushions, meditating, chanting, charging our spiritual batteries. Then we go out into the world and deal with whatever awaits us. Afterward, we return to our cushions and regain our spiritual strength.

This ebb and flow between the spiritual and the conventional is the stuff that life is made of, and as we become more attuned to that flow, the transition becomes easier until one day it disappears completely. On that day, there's nothing spiritual or conventional in the world. There's just life, and we're able to live it fully every day.

**Lesson:** When life gives you a mess, clean it up.

# Suffering Is Caused by Desire

# Hungry Wolves and Desire

Two hungry wolves were standing on top of a mountain, and down in the valley below they spotted a herd of elk. The younger wolf looked over at his older friend and said, "Hey, let's run down into the valley and eat one of those elk." But the older wolf just smiled and said, "No, my friend. Let's make a plan, walk down there, and eat them all."

The lesson is straight-forward. If we rush headlong into things, we'll get limited results. But if we take our time and plan, we'll get everything we want. It makes sense on the surface, but there's one glaring issue. It's completely wrong.

Planning is good. Taking our time is good. But it doesn't matter how carefully we plan or how slowly we move in the end. No one gets to have it all. This is the truth of life.

That's why the second noble truth states that suffering is caused by desire because there will always be something more just out of reach. Maybe we're happily married, but we still think about the "one that got away." Perhaps we have a steady job, but we long to write the great American novel. Or our wish to travel the world is hampered by responsibilities that force us to stay home.

The human brain is very good at coming up with "one more thing" that we need to be happy. But this constant desire for new things and experiences results in us feeling empty, lost, and disappointed despite the many blessings that we possess.

The road to happiness is paved with moments of acceptance. And part of that is learning to accept that there are things in life that we'll never have. But this doesn't have to be a reason for sadness. On the contrary, not having it all can be a source of great peace.

When we stop thinking about "the one that got away," we're able to focus on the one that's here right now. And giving up our dream to travel the world allows us to make the most of life at home. The beauty of life is in the gaps, in the things we'll never have.

That's why Buddhism teaches us to regulate our desires. Not because they're wrong but because turning away from desire helps us live life more fully, without regrets. In the end, we realize that we're not slaves to our inclinations, and we can choose how we live in the world.

In that moment, we don't need to run down the mountain. And we don't need to walk down either. Instead, we can remain at the summit and appreciate the view.

**Lesson:** Desire brings us suffering. Acceptance brings us peace.

## Endless Wanting

Some Buddhist authors like to soften the second noble truth by changing the word "desire" to "craving" or "clinging." The implication being that some desire is okay if we don't take it too far. And while it's true that craving and clinging accentuate our suffering, we can't ignore the fact that the root cause of our existential pain is desire.

We suffer because we want things we don't have. And we suffer because we want to keep things that inevitably go away. One might argue that desire is a natural part of life, and it is. But that's why the first noble truth states that suffering is also a natural part of life. The two go together like peanut butter and jelly. Early in life, I worked hard to fulfill my desires. I believed that if I had a bit more money, a better education, or a faster car, all my problems would be ended. I'll give you one guess how that turned out.

Next, I discovered Buddhism, and my desires changed. I didn't want money anymore. I wanted enlightenment. Of course, no one seemed to know what enlightenment entailed, but all the guys with robes and cool titles like Roshi and Sensei told me that it was great.

To be fair, my life did get better during this time, and I learned that some desires are less painful than others. But as time passed, I felt like there was a hole in my life, one that couldn't be filled by enlightenment.

It's hard to describe this feeling that I had, that I still have in my weaker moments, other than to say I felt like a giant puzzle. And I was complete except for one piece that was missing from the center. Not having that piece of the puzzle was killing me. So, I searched everywhere for it. I looked in relationships, I looked in my job, and I spent an excessive amount of time looking in Buddhist books. But it was nowhere to be found.

Then something shifted. During my meditations, I stopped trying to control my thoughts, and I simply observed. Slowly, I started to realize that my thoughts and emotions are not me. Anger arises from somewhere. And if I allow it, anger passes away. The same is true of sadness, fear, and even my desire.

I don't know where this endless wanting comes from, this feeling that things aren't quite right. But I do know that if I sit with it for a while, neither grasping at it nor pushing it away, then the wanting returns to whence it came. And I'm left with a feeling of peace.

Because there's no missing puzzle piece. And there's no great mystery to solve. I'm perfect and complete exactly as I am. The world is perfect and complete exactly as it is. And my practice is learning to accept that fact regardless of what desire tells me.

**Lesson:** Everything we need is already right here.

## A Car Ride to Nowhere

At any given moment, we are experiencing two different versions of the world. There is the world as it is. And on top of that, there is a conceptual overlay, which represents the world as we want it to be. The more these two world views align, the happier and more peaceful our lives become. The more they separate, the more agitated we become.

Everyone understands this on an instinctual level. That's why we spend so much time, money, and resources trying to make the world line up with the way we think it should be. We make schedules, we send reminders, and we make backup plans all in the hope that life will cooperate with our desires.

Unfortunately, things rarely happen exactly as we want them too. Life doesn't care about our schedules, it doesn't read our reminders, and it laughs at our backup plans. This can be a great source of suffering if we aren't careful. Further, it can create the illusion of problems that aren't there.

Case in point, several years ago I had just started a new job as a business analyst for a software company, and I was eager to make a good impression. Things had been going smoothly for several weeks, my boss was happy with my performance, and I was gaining lots of useful experience.

Eventually, I was entrusted to lead a big project that had been in the works for some time. There were a lot of eyes on me as I'd be working with essential clients along with reporting my progress back to our department director. But if I did well, the sky was the limit in terms of my career.

So, I scheduled a kickoff meeting that would involve my boss along with all the project stakeholders. It would be an opportunity for everyone to meet face to face and hear my vision in of how the project would go.

I spent weeks building a slide deck that would lay out my proposed changes along with the expected benefits. I practiced my "pitch" on some of my friends to ensure that it was equal measures professional and convincing. And I triple-checked my numbers to ensure that they were correct.

On the day of the meeting, I left home 30 minutes earlier than usual just in case something unexpected happened. Everything was going well until I turned onto the one-way street that led to my office buildings and ran into a two-mile long line of cars that was moving at the pace of a geriatric snail.

I would find out later that the slowdown was due to construction work that was being done to fix a broken water main. Unfortunately, there was only one road leading into the office park where my company was located, so I had no choice but to wait in line with everyone else.

"No worries," I thought to myself, "I won't have time for one more practice session before the meeting, but I won't be late." However, my optimism slowly started to sour as time passed. It had been 7:15 a.m. when I turned onto the street. At 7:45 a.m. I had only moved about 0.5 miles. My meeting was at 8 a.m.

Panic started to well up inside me as the minutes continued to tick off the clock. By 7:50 a.m. I was freaking out. At this point, I could see my office building in the distance, but I couldn't get to it! For a moment, I thought about abandoning my car and trying to run to the meeting, but even in my frantic state, I knew that leaving my car in the middle of the road wasn't an option.

"I'm going to be late," I thought to myself. "My boss is never going to trust me again. What if she fires me?!"

Instinctively I started to focus on my breathing. As I noticed the feeling of the air moving in and out of my lungs along with the sensation of my chest expanding and contracting, my heart rate slowed.

I was still upset, but the exercise created a tiny bit of space between me and my emotions, allowing me to take stock of my situation. I was sitting in an air-conditioned car with my favorite radio station playing. There was plenty of food in my refrigerator, and my cat loved me. I was OK.

"I'm OK, I'm OK," I repeated the words to myself like a mantra. I looked at the clock again. It read 7:58 a.m. There was no getting around it; I was going to miss the meeting. There was nothing left to do but face the music.

I pulled out my cell phone and called my boss to let her know the situation. About 30 seconds into my explanation/apology about what happened, she cut me off and started laughing. She'd just got off the phone with our clients; they were stuck in the same traffic jam that I was in!

She'd been calling the attendees to let them know the meeting was being rescheduled, and I'd been the last person on her list. We had a good laugh regarding the whole situation, and then I let her go, so she could continue making calls.

Looking back on that situation, I now realize that the real source of my suffering wasn't the construction or the traffic jam. It was me. More specifically, it was the fantasies that I created in my head around what would happen if I was late for the meeting and my desire to have everything go as planned.

Technically, I wasn't even late when I called my boss to tell her what had happened, but my desire blinded me to the reality of the situation. The only thing I could see was how I wanted the world to be, and I wasn't willing to accept the world as it was.

The gap between my desire (e.g., the way I wanted the world to be) and reality (e.g., the way the world was) resulted in a considerable amount of mental pain on my part. And that suffering didn't help the situation. It didn't fix the broken water main or make the traffic move faster.

It just made me miserable. More than that, it caused me to freak out over a problem that wasn't a problem!

Of course, this doesn't mean that we shouldn't try hard at things or make plans. But it does mean that we need to be reasonable in our expectations. We need to make plans from a place of acceptance, with an understanding that things may go awry. We need to be flexible and adjust our desires to the realities of life in any given moment. Doing so allows us to make new plans from a place of peace, not agitation.

The one thing we can count on in life is that things will go wrong. We'll get stuck in traffic jams at the worst possible time, the barista will screw up our order, and people will disappoint us. But that's OK.

Because if the first noble truth reminds us that life rarely goes as planned, then the second noble truth tells us that we have a choice. We can choose not to suffer or at least to suffer less. And we make this choice each time we adjust our desires to the reality of our situation.

In this way, a healthy tension develops between our desires and the world. We try for things, stuff happens, and then we adjust and try again. There's no stress involved because we accept that our plans will probably have to change.

Eventually, we stop fighting with life, and we learn to flow with it instead. Like a leaf floating down a river we bump into rocks, we go around them, and we continue on our path. If we get stuck behind a log and need to stop along the way, that's OK, too.

We accept the good things in life, and we accept the not-so-good things as well. Because even if we don't get where we want to go, we know we'll end up where we belong.

**Lesson:** Life is a river; go with the flow.

## The Three Poisons

In the original Pali, the word for desire is *Tanha,* which can also be translated as either craving or thirst. So, from the Buddhist perspective, all humans suffer from an unquenchable thirst, and our attempts to quench that thirst through either status, experiences, or material possessions result in suffering.

In his wisdom, Buddha divided our desire into three categories that simultaneously feed off each other and serve as a significant cause of suffering both for ourselves and other living beings. As a result of the evil fruit that comes from each of these categories, he called them "The Three Poisons," and they are as follows:

**Greed -** The desire for things that we do not have

**Anger/Aversion -** The desire to get rid of things that we possess

**Ignorance -** The desire for things to remain as they are although all things are impermanent

All the pain and heartache that exists in our world (e.g., war, poverty, thievery, etc.) can be traced back to one or more of the three poisons. That's why the second and third noble truths name desire as the cause of our suffering and the ending of craving as a cure for it. However, the issue is a bit more nuanced than it might seem.

For example, if we contemplate the conventional thirst for water that humans experience, we can easily see that this desire exists on a spectrum. So, if someone hasn't had a drink of water for several hours after laboring in the hot sun, they would probably experience some discomfort. However, since it's only been a few hours since their last drink of water that person's overall suffering would be low.

But if that same person were forced to go several days without water, they would experience a very intense level of discomfort; their suffering would be much more significant. They would have dry mouth, headaches from dehydration, and they'd probably be at risk for organ failure. So, from this example, we can see that the level of a person's suffering due to physical thirst is directly related to how thirsty they've become.

High levels of thirst result in high levels of suffering, and smaller levels of thirst result in relatively small levels of suffering.

This is also true of the existential thirst/ desire that we discuss in Buddhism. However, our level of desire doesn't change as a result of the amount of time since we last accumulated an object or experience. Instead, it varies based on our level of attachment to the object of our desire.

Attachment increases our level of desire, which increases the potential for suffering. For example, let's say that a person desires to have $1 million in their bank account. They have lots of ideas on how they'd spend the money, and it would be life changing for them if that happened. If that person has a relatively low amount of attachment to that desire, the level of suffering that results from it will also be low.

On the other hand, if that same person has a very high level of attachment to that desire, to the point that they are willing to steal or even kill other people for it, then the potential for suffering is exceptionally high.

As the level of attachment to a specific desire increases, the desire itself also increases, and the result is greater misery both for the individual and the people around them.

That's why Buddhism teaches *non-attachment,* which allows us to live with our desires without them controlling us. When we practice non-attachment, we live in a world where we work for things to happen while simultaneously practicing acceptance toward the fact that we may not get what we want. The more we practice non-attachment, the less power our desires have over us, and the less suffering we cause for ourselves and others. This practice also lessens the role that the three poisons (greed, anger, and ignorance) play in our daily lives.

Thus, if desire is the cause of human suffering, then non-attachment is the cause of inner peace. And the more time we spend practicing non-attachment in daily life, the closer we move to *nirvana.*

Nirvana is a Sanskrit word that means to blow out. Of course, this begs the question "What are we blowing out?" And the answer is the three poisons of greed, anger, and delusion. An easy way to think of it is to imagine the three poisons as fires that are burning us alive from the inside out.

However, instead of kerosene, each fire is being fueled by our desires. More desires result in bigger flames and more suffering. Fewer desires result in smaller flames and less suffering. So, the more we practice non-attachment and acceptance in our daily lives, the less suffering we have, and the more peaceful our lives become.

This peaceful state of mind, free of the three poisons, is what's known as nirvana. However, it isn't a duality. Instead, nirvana exists on a spectrum, and we move deeper into it or farther out from it depending on our daily actions.

An example would be a monastic who has lived a virtuous life that was rooted in the practices of nonattachment and acceptance. Through his actions, he will have built up great trust with the lay community around him, set a good example, provided spiritual counsel, and created relationships where the community is happy to support him with food, medicine, shelter, and clothing.

As a result, he lives deeply in nirvana, free of desirous attachments, because he knows that his needs will be met.

The situation is slightly different for lay Buddhists, but the general idea is the same. As we continue to perform virtuous acts in daily life that are in keeping with the Noble eight-fold path, we create the conditions for our needs to be met. We also weaken the grip that greed, anger, and ignorance have on our lives.

Every time we work hard at our job, show kindness to our family and friends, or practice meditation we move deeper into nirvana and reduce suffering for ourselves and others.

**Lesson:** Virtuous Action + Non-Attachment = Nirvana

# Taming the Monkey-Mind

Indigenous hunters on the continent of Africa have developed a technique for capturing baboons. They'll wait until the baboon is watching, and then they'll dig a tiny hole into the side of a giant ant hill. After that, they'll place some sweet-smelling melon seeds into the hole and walk away.

Overcome with curiosity, the baboon saunters over and sticks his hand in the hole. Then he makes a fist to grab the seeds and pull them out. But he can't get his hand out of the hole!

His balled-up fist is too full, and it won't fit. Of course, he could just let go of the seeds and walk away. But his desire to eat them is so great that he's unwilling to do this. Instead, he tires himself out trying to pull his clenched fist from the ant hill. He remains in this sorry state until the hunter comes to collect him.[2]

In many ways, human beings are like the baboon in this story. When we have a strong wish for something, our emotions can blind us to the ill effects of that desire. As a result, we find ourselves clinging to the very things that cause us pain. Of course, we could end our suffering by merely letting go of the objects that we crave, but the thought never occurs to us.

That's why Buddhist teachers warn students about the monkey-mind and the importance of taming it. Because when humans have a monkey-mind that's full of desire and continually chasing after things, they often create problems for themselves and others. These problems occur because the monkey-mind keeps us from clearly seeing the *karma* of our actions.

Simply put, karma is the way that cause and effect play out in daily life. So, if we throw a baseball up into the air, that's a cause. And the effect is that it will eventually fall back down to earth. Parents have an intuitive understanding of karma. That's why they don't allow children to throw balls in the house. The cause of a child throwing things in the house may result in the effect of a broken window!

The teaching of karma is simple. However, it's challenging to put into practice. Our monkey-minds keep us from seeing the karmic causes and effects that we create in daily life. Blinded by desire, we fall into unskillful habits that make life more complicated than it needs to be.

That's why Buddhist training is so important. The practices of meditation and moral discipline allows us to tame our monkey-minds and see the karma of our actions more clearly. With a calm mind, we can then make better choices that result in less suffering for ourselves and others.

Without this training, however, we can end up like the baboon in the story - trapped by our desires as the hunter closes in.

**Lesson:** Stop monkeying around, and just let go!

# The Way to End Suffering
# Is to End Desire

# An Angry Office Meltdown

When I started practicing Buddhism in 2013, one of the things that got me hooked was the grim nature of the stories that I read. Students were getting smacked by their teachers, people realized enlightenment by stubbing their toe, and hermit monks had their huts burned down by angry old ladies.

The general message was always something along the lines of "Life sucks, but here are some helpful ways to deal with it." And that appealed to me because I was broke, my personal life was in shambles, and I went to bed each night feeling miserable. In short, my life sucked back then, but it felt good to find a spiritual practice that didn't sugarcoat that fact.

Instead, Buddhism gave me a tool in seated meditation that allowed me to look at my life from a distance, investigate why everything was going wrong, and try to make better decisions. It wasn't easy. There were days when sitting on the cushion felt like torture. But I always felt better when I finished.

So, I kept going. I learned a lot about myself and the world in general, but the biggest lesson that I learned is that most negative emotions (fear, anger, sadness, etc.) come from wanting something from life and then not getting it.

Furthermore, if we can train ourselves to stop wanting those things and become happy with what we have, life becomes more peaceful. There was an incident early in my career that hammered this point home for me.

At the time, I was a middle manager in a call center. I worked with a team of call center representatives who took calls from our installation technicians, keeping track of what was installed in the customers' homes and accepting payment for any additional equipment that was purchased.

For my part, I was there to make sure people showed up on time, make the schedule, and to answer any questions the installation technicians might have. Things were running smoothly until a new manager named Mark was hired to help me cover the department. Mark and I had been good friends before he joined the team, so I was happy to have him as a co-manager. But my attitude changed after a few weeks of our working together.

Mark had ideas around running the department, and I had completely different views. Coincidentally, a new call center director was hired right around the same time that this was happening, and he tended to like Mark's opinions more than mine.

So, in the span of a few weeks, I went from being able to run my department exactly like I wanted to explaining every management decision that I made at our weekly meetings. Sadly, words like "compromise" and "calm down" weren't in my vocabulary back then. So, Mark and I argued a lot, about everything.

After one especially heated disagreement, I stormed back to my cubicle full of self-righteous fury and started slamming things around on my desk. I'd only been meditating for a few months at that point, but I knew enough to know that I should at least take a few calming breaths before I annihilated my workstation.

While doing that, I noticed something about my anger. It didn't feel good. My shoulders hurt from being hunched over. My head ached. My heart was racing. And to top it all off, I'd managed to spill coffee on my keyboard.

Why was I doing this to myself? Asking myself that question allowed me to calm down and take in my surroundings. I looked around and saw Mark joking with the other managers. Mark didn't care that I was angry. Next, I looked at the phone reps. They were all diligently hunched over, entering data into their computers. The phone reps didn't care that I was angry.

Finally, I looked out the window. The sun was setting behind some office buildings in the distance just as it had done countless times before. Life was moving forward just like it always had. And the only person that was suffering due to my anger was me.

Coming to this realization was empowering because it reminded me that the only thing I could control was myself. I was angry because I wanted complete control of my department, and life wasn't giving me that anymore. But once I accepted the fact that life (and Mark) didn't care what I wanted, I stopped expecting to get anything from them.

Instead, I learned to focus less on the things that I desired and more on the things that I could control (making suitable recommendations for the department, coming to work on time, being polite to my employees, etc.), and I did my best to stop worrying about the things that I couldn't control. Doing otherwise only caused me more suffering without changing the situation.

It's been several years since I had that realization, and this way of thinking hasn't wholly cured me of my negative emotions (fear, anger, sadness, etc.). But I've noticed that focusing only on the things that I can control causes my mood to level out much faster than it once did. Also, I'm able to live with more openness and compassion because I'm not so afraid of what will happen from one moment to the next.

In the end, I know that something will happen. Maybe it will be what I want, and maybe it won't. But my practice is adjusting my desires to the reality of each moment. If certain things are out of my hands, the only thing I can do is practice acceptance and focus on other things.

Honestly, I want more certainty than that. I want to feel like the whole world is subject to my will, and nothing unexpected will ever happen. But life doesn't care what I want. It just gives me what it gives me. And I've learned to be OK with that.

**Lesson:** If something is outside of your control, accept it and move on.


## Plant-Based Buddhism

"Should Buddhists eat meat?" is a question that I get a lot. With its emphasis on non-violence and the interconnectedness of all things, it's understandable that people would assume that all Buddhists are either vegan or vegetarian. And while it's true that every Buddhist must wrestle with their desire for meat and the suffering that's caused by that desire, the reality is more complicated than a simple yes or no.

First, we need to establish that there isn't just one Buddhism. Rather, there are many Buddhist traditions that vary in how they express the Dharma in much the same way that there are many denominations of Christianity. These different traditions vary based on culture, geography, and openness to change. As a result, policies on food choices vary quite a bit.

The historical Buddha was not vegan or vegetarian. He was a wandering monastic who only ate the food that was offered to him by the lay community. Naturally, one can't be too picky when they only eat what is donated, so his practice involved accepting all donations with sincere gratitude.

However, he did place some rules around meat consumption for him and his monastics. They were not allowed to eat meat if the animal was killed within their sight or hearing. They also couldn't accept meat if they suspected the animal was killed specifically for them.

Furthermore, animal butchery is one of the forbidden professions under the tenet of Right Livelihood in the Noble Eightfold Path. This suggests that Buddha did not see any adverse karmic effects in the consumption of meat in and of itself. However, he did see issues with the actual killing of animals for food.

If the animal was already dead, it could be eaten because it could no longer suffer, however, monastics were not allowed to encourage or take part in the killing of animals because then they'd be subject to the adverse karmic effects. This is confirmed in the Sutta-Nipata where the

Buddha reminds his students that it's their actions, not their birth, that makes them holy men and women by stating the following:

> *Whoever having laid aside violence in respect of all beings, moving or still, does not kill or cause to kill him, I call a brahman*[3]

As a result, Theravadin Buddhist monks in places like Sri Lanka and Thailand still engage in this tradition of gratefully accepting both meat and vegetable offerings from the public if no animals were killed within their sight or hearing, and they don't suspect the animal was killed specifically for them.

The practice changes, however, in the Vajrayana tradition that is practiced in Tibet and Nepal. In those areas, monastics eat quite a bit of meat, mostly yak, and very few vegetables. This is because that part of the world is mountainous with poor soil, so plant agriculture is difficult. However, they work to cleanse any negative karma by engaging in rigorous liturgies of chanting and prayer before and after meals.

In contrast, the Mahayana Buddhist tradition in places like Korea, Japan, and China places a considerable emphasis on eating a plant-based diet. In fact, vegan and vegetarian cooking are ritualized in Japan through the practice of Shojin Ryori, which requires practitioners to hand-pick vegetables at the market, prepare a meal without the use of modern tools, and then present the dish in a way that is both delicious and visually appealing.[4]

Additionally, the Korean Buddhist nun Jeong Kwan has made quite the name for herself by traveling the world, sharing traditional vegan temple cuisine with the world. In an interview with South China Morning Post, Jeong Kwan had this to say about her cooking:

> *What makes Korean temple food special is the energy channeled to the food. As food is a pathway to enlightenment, it does not have to be sophisticated or obsessed with taste.*[5]

This statement reflects the overall feeling in Mahayana Buddhism that every facet of life (working, sleeping, eating, etc.) must be a reflection of enlightened behavior. This differs from Theravadin Buddhism, which draws a clear distinction between spiritual practice and daily life.

For a Theravadin monk who is either accepting food donations or having meals prepared for him, the focus is on gratefully accepting the donations. However, Mahayana Buddhists are expected to be more self-sufficient, often growing their own crops and preparing their own food. As a result, they've developed practices like ritualized vegan cooking that help them change mundane tasks into vehicles for spiritual practice.

Additionally, Zen Buddhist temples in places like China, Japan, and Korea often receive cash donations from parishioners that they use to purchase food for the temple. So, there is a direct karmic link between them and any animal that is butchered on their behalf. That's why Zen Master Thich Thanh Tu had this to say on the issue of eating animals:

> *There are three ways of killing that we, as Buddhists, have to restrain: either by directly killing, indirectly killing, or rejoicing to see others be killed. Not only does this apply to human life, it should also be extended to all living beings.* [6]

All of this is to say that there's no single, right answer to the question "Should Buddhists eat meat?" It depends mainly on the tradition, geography, and lifestyle (lay vs. monastic) of each practitioner. However, the crux of my training has been in the Zen and Pureland Buddhist traditions. And after attending several meditation retreats where I lived healthily without eating meat, I chose to transition to a plant-based lifestyle.

I did this for several reasons. First, I feel very fortunate to have been born in the United States where I have things like air conditioning, indoor plumbing, and Wi-Fi. So, not eating meat is an ascetic practice for me. It's a way to take a little bit less from the world and say, "thank you" for the many gifts that I've received.

Also, living in a capitalist system means that there's a direct karmic link between my purchases and the suffering that's caused by them. Unfortunately, I can't end all suffering; the first noble truth makes that clear. However, I can make food choices that reduce suffering for myself and others.

When I compared the level of suffering involved in plant agriculture to the level of suffering involved in animal agriculture, plant agriculture seemed to cause the least amount of harm to the planet, animals, and human beings. So, I decided to get my calories strictly from plants. I also refrain from wearing products like fur, wool, and leather for the same reason.

Finally, I think the biggest reason is that I couldn't find a justifiable reason not to do it. I'm not a Theravadin monk who lives in poverty and gratefully accepts donations. And I'm not in a situation like the Vajrayana monks of Tibet and Nepal where I risk starvation if I don't eat animal products.

I'm a Westerner who receives a paycheck every two weeks and buys his food at a grocery store. Once I established that I could be physically healthy without animal products, the only reason not to do it was a lingering desire for meat. However, the third noble truth is clear that the way to end suffering is to end desire. So, I made giving up my desire for these things part of my spiritual practice.

Should other Buddhists do the same? I don't know. That's for them to decide based on the circumstances in their lives and their understanding of the sutras. However, it does fall on each of us to investigate the karma that's associated with our desires and make choices that benefit both ourselves and all sentient beings.

**Lesson:** We must investigate our desires and strive to make better choices.

## Freedom and Meditation

One of the nicknames that often gets thrown around when people describe America is "The Land of the Free." Of course, that begs the question "What does it mean to be free?" The dictionary defines freedom in the following ways:

1. the state of being free or at liberty rather than in confinement
2. exemption from external control, interference, regulation, etc.
3. the power to determine action without constraint[7]

These are solid definitions, but they're a bit academic. So, I did an extremely unscientific, informal survey of my close friends, and the general agreement was that freedom is the ability to do whatever you want. Honestly, that's what I expected them to say as it's entirely in keeping with the American ethos around wealth and prosperity.

We spend huge chunks of our lives working to accumulate enough status and money to do whatever we want. We earn expensive degrees, we go after jobs with impressive titles, and we buy things in the hopes that we'll be able to move freely through the world.

That's all fine on the surface, but there's a problem. None of us can "determine action without constraint" or "be exempt from external control." After all, the government enacts laws that restrict our movements, we're constantly constrained by our bodies' physical limitations, and responsibilities to family interfere with our personal choices. In short, it doesn't matter how much wealth or status we possess. No one gets to do whatever they want. None of us are truly free.

What's interesting about the idea of freedom is that if anyone could have achieved it through conventional means, it would have been Buddha. He was born a Hindu prince, and his father gave him the best of everything. He had access to the tastiest foods, the finest teachers, wealth, and beautiful women. He should've been the happiest, freest man on earth. But he wasn't. In fact, he was so unhappy that he left all of his wealth and good fortune behind in the middle of the night and devoted the rest of his life to spiritual practice.

In his lifetime, the Buddha determined that there are eight types of suffering that humans experience, that are completely inescapable by conventional means. They are birth, aging, sickness, death, losing friends, encountering enemies, not finding what one wants, finding what one does not want.[8] Furthermore, he established that our desire to escape these experiences only causes us to suffer more.

That's why Buddhism teaches us to seek freedom not by fulfilling our desires, but by learning to let them go. In this way, we're able to experience a different kind of liberation, one that doesn't hinge on our ability to move without restriction or not be subject laws.

One of the ways that we can find the liberation that Buddhism describes is through the act of seated meditation. We sit on the cushion, cross our legs, and resolve not to move a muscle until the timer goes off. On the surface, this seems like one of the most unfree actions that a person can take, and that's what makes it so hard.

But if we stick with it, then something magical happens. As we sit there unable to check our phones, or buy things online, or even scratch our nose, we learn that we can be perfectly happy without those things. We may go back to them when the meditation ends, but for that brief period we become bigger and more special than our hobbies and possessions.

We find freedom that's not based on anything outside of ourselves, which means it can never be taken away. And that's the difference between conventional freedom and Buddhist freedom. Conventional freedom is fragile because it's built on impermanent people, places, and things. On the other hand, Buddhist freedom is strong because it's built on the letting go of those things.

Meditation is the physical embodiment of that letting go process. Whether we sit on the cushion for one minute or one hour, we're forced to "let go" of our desires repeatedly. Each time we want to reach for our phones and choose not to, each time we want to give in to anger, but turn our attention to our breath instead, we train ourselves not to be slaves to our every whim.

Eventually, we reach a state where we have nothing left to fear because we have nothing left to lose. We've already let it all go. In that moment, we move deeper into the lasting freedom and perfect peace that is nirvana.

**Lesson:** Letting go is the path to perfect freedom

## Zen and the Art of Kindness

The third noble truth states that the way to end suffering is to end desire. This is an accurate assessment and a good first step in understanding the teaching. But there is a second half. Sometimes, our lack of desire can also be a cause of suffering. For example, there are many times in life when we don't desire to do certain things even when we know they'll benefit ourselves and others. I experienced this early in my practice when I was learning how to bow.

Bowing at the waist or doing a full prostration, which involves going from a standing position to having one's forehead touch the floor is a major part of Buddhist practice. In fact, a proper bow is seen as the embodiment of humility, a literal shrinking of the physical self in deference to the universe.

Buddhists are expected to be very good at bowing. We bow to the cushion before and after meditation. We bow to statues of the Buddha, and we bow to each other. There are even stories of Zen patriarchs who regularly bowed to cats and dogs. That being said, I had great difficulty with bowing early in my practice.

I felt vulnerable and defensive each time I placed my forehead on the floor. Why was I showing so much deference to a teacher (Buddha) who'd been dead for over 2,000 years? Why was I expected to show respect to my fellow students when I barely knew them? It all seemed strange to me, and a bit silly.

But it was an important part of Buddhist ritual, and no one (not even my fragile ego) was more important than that. My teacher was patient, but he made it clear that if I wanted to participate, I needed to bow alongside everyone else. So, I did it. Grudgingly, haltingly, I placed my forehead on the ground.

Initially, I did this purely out of respect for the ritual. I wanted to practice Buddhism, and this was part of it. If I didn't like that, I could try something else. I thought about it several times - trying something else. But I never did. To this day, I don't know why that is. I just know that I kept showing up to the temple, and I kept bowing despite my misgivings.

After a few years, my discomfort was replaced with habit. I stopped analyzing everything, and I simply did what was expected. When the ritual required that I bow at the waist to another student, I did. When the ritual required that I do a full prostration to the Buddha, I did.

I valued the comfort of my sangha and the continuity of ritual more than my ego, so I did what was needed. But I still didn't want to do it. The benefits of bowing had been explained to me, and I understood them intellectually. But the desire just wasn't there. There were two events. However, that changed everything.

The first event happened at CloudWater Zendo, the Zen Center of Cleveland during a chanting service. We were chanting the heart sutra (something I've done a million times) and one of the female monks, Ven. Shih Ming-Xing, stood up to prostrate before the Buddha (something I've seen a million times), but this was different. When her forehead touched the floor the monk, the Buddha, and the Heart Sutra all became one thing.

From this kneeling position her arms spread outwards like bird wings, tracing half circles toward the altar, the motion ended with her palms raised upwards above her head in supplication. I don't remember her getting up. One moment she was kneeling on the ground, the next she was standing before the altar, rooted there like some auspicious Buddhist tree. And then it was over. She returned to her place in the meditation hall, and practice continued as if nothing happened.

The next event happened during my lay minister induction ceremony at the Bright Dawn Center of Oneness Buddhism. The ceremony had ended, and everyone was taking turns paying their final respects to the Buddha while the newly minted Buddhist teachers stood to the side.

One woman stepped in front of the altar, smiled as if she were meeting an old friend, and bowed at the waist. It was the most natural and joyful thing I've ever seen. No words were spoken, but it felt like she and Buddha had a nice little chat. Then she straightened up, nodded as if to say, "goodbye," and walked away.

Two women, one practice, so many lessons; the monk embodied the stillness of the absolute with her bow. And the laywoman embodied the cheerfulness of the conventional with hers. As I reflected on my bowing practice, I wondered if I could manifest the Dharma in the same way that they did. I wondered what would happen if I put my everything into each bow regardless of my mood or desire to do so. I didn't know the answer. But I was willing to try.

Things were shaky in the beginning. The first time I tried to give 100 percent during a prostration I headbutted the floor so hard that Ven. Shih Ying-Fa, the abbot of CloudWater Zendo, the Zen Center of Cleveland looked over to see if I was OK. But I stuck with it, and I improved over time.

As I did this, something changed within me. Each time I prostrated before Buddha; my hands raised in supplication; my heart softened a little bit. Every time I bowed to a fellow student; I became more trusting. Yes, the practice did make me vulnerable in a very real, physical sense of the word. But that was OK.

Bowing taught me that being vulnerable is okay. I can open myself up to the world, and nothing bad will happen, even if I do headbutt the floor. As I've slowly improved in the art of bowing, I've looked for other opportunities to embody this lesson in daily life. One of the ways that I've found is through expressing kindness toward strangers and people I dislike.

The practice of kindness is very similar to the practice of bowing. It's an important part of Buddhist practice, and there are many reasons why we should engage in it. But being kind to others isn't always easy. It makes us feel vulnerable. That's why we reserve it for people we trust.

We're kind to family and friends because we have a reasonable belief that they'll be kind to us. But we're unkind or neutral toward people we don't see as trustworthy for fear that we'll be hurt. In other words, we lack the desire to show kindness to others for the same reason that we may not want to bow in the meditation hall.

But if we treat the act of kindness as a part of the ritual of daily life (just like bowing is part of the ritual of Buddhism), then we can do it regardless of how we feel.

We "bow" each time we smile at a coworker after a disagreement. We bow each time we call a friend who we haven't spoken with in a while. And we bow each time we respond to difficult situations with kindness instead of anger.

This can be a difficult practice. In fact, it may be physically painful at times as we humble ourselves to the universe. However, each time we do it our hearts soften a little bit, and we become more trusting. Of course, things won't always go as planned, and there will be times that we make mistakes or end up feeling disappointed in the results.

But if we stick with it, then every bow will embody the stillness of the absolute. And every kind act will show the cheerfulness of the conventional; until we lose ourselves completely in the wonderful ritual of life.

**Lesson:** All of Buddha's teachings live in a single act of kindness


## A Buddhist Take on New Year's Resolutions

There was an old Buddhist priest who ran a small temple at the top of a hillside. He'd spent several decades chanting, praying, and providing spiritual support to his community, but the time had come for him to retire. Sadly, the priest did not have any children that he could give the temple too.

So, he put together a small wooden sign and placed it in front of a withered, crooked tree that was growing outside the gates of his temple. The sign said, "Anyone who can tell me how to fix this tree can have my temple and the land that it resides on."

Word spread quickly about the sign, and people came from all over the country to offer advice. Some told the priest that he should cut the tree down. Others suggested the use of wires and ropes to straighten its branches.

The old priest listened patiently to each person, and when they finished, he grabbed a frying pan and chased each one from the temple grounds. Many years passed, and it started to seem like no one would be able to answer the priest's koan. Finally, a Buddhist nun appeared at the temple. She'd been traveling for many days, and she needed a place to rest. She knocked on the temple gates, and after a few moments the priest came out, frying pan in hand.

"I'm very tired," the nun said. "May I sleep at your temple tonight?"

"No, you can't sleep at my temple tonight," the priest replied, "but you can have my temple and land it resides on if you can answer one question."

"OK," the nun replied calmly, "What's your question?

The priest pointed at the crooked tree with his frying pan and said, "How do I fix this tree?"

Upon hearing this, the nun looked at the tree for a long time. She noticed the trunk was so bent that it almost ran parallel with the ground. She saw the gnarled branches that twisted in strange directions, and the dead leaves that surrounded the tree's base.

Eventually, the nun turned to the priest and said, "Just leave it alone; the tree is fine the way it is." As soon as the nun finished speaking the old priest smiled broadly and dropped his frying pan. He bowed deeply to the nun, and said, "Follow me, this temple belongs to you." [9]

At the end of every year, my timeline fills with people discussing their New Year's resolutions. Words like "New Year, New You!" and "Get beach body ready!" fill my screen like mantras, representing the hopes of people who want to be smarter, richer, and prettier in 2019.

This is to be expected. After all, our economy hinges on the idea that if we buy one more gym membership or add one more mindfulness app to our phone, our dreams will come true. But each time one of these messages appears I think back to the tree in the story, and I wonder, "What if we're not as broken as we think we are?"

To be sure, each of us is a "crooked tree" dealing with our own fears and insecurities. Our bodies don't look the way we think they should, our paychecks don't have enough zeroes, and our relationships aren't what we desire. But why is that a bad thing?

After all, the tree in the story was gnarled and ugly. But the tree accepted its crooked nature. The priest accepted its crooked nature, and everything was peaceful as a result. The only time fear or anxiety entered the picture was when foolish monks attempted to make the crooked tree straight. That's why the priest chased them off with a frying pan.

In contrast, the nun looked at the tree, and she saw what it was, not what she desired it to be. She understood that whatever made it crooked and gnarled could not have happened any other way. Thus, the tree could not exist in any other way. She understood that the tree could not be fixed because the tree was never broken.

What would happen if we looked at ourselves like the nun looked at that tree? What would happen if we treasured our imperfections in the same way that the priest treasured the tree's gnarled branches? I think our lives would be better as a result. More than that, I think it's incumbent on us to see the perfection of our imperfect souls.

Buddhism can be helpful in this regard. When done correctly, without nonsense words like "self-improvement" or "enlightenment," the practice helps us see past our thoughts about how life should be. When we sit on cushions that are always either too hard or too soft, we understand the perfect nature of imperfect cushions. When we mix-up words during chants, we understand the perfect nature of imperfect chanting. And that understanding bleeds over into the rest of our lives.

Eventually, we step on the scale and see the perfection of our imperfect weight. And we enjoy the perfect chaos of our imperfect home life. And we exist in a state of peace, rejoicing in the great perfection of our messy, crooked lives. Because crooked trees/people are perfectly crooked, and we suffer when we try to make them straight.

So, I toyed with the idea of not making a New Year's resolution. The idea of people spending days or even weeks combing their imperfections to find something to "fix" made my heart hurt. And I didn't want to participate in that.

But I decided that it would be best to engage with the perfect nature of this imperfect ritual. So, I made a single New Year's resolution that goes as follows: This year I'll wake up every morning, I'll go to sleep every night, and I'll live my crooked life in between.

**Lesson:** We must enjoy the perfection of our crookedness

# The Way to End Desire Is the Eightfold Path

# Many Ways to Do It

In 2014, I had been practicing Buddhism on my own for a year. I was meditating regularly, studying Buddhist texts, and generally feeling a lot better about life. Things were far from perfect, but I finally felt like my life was moving in the right direction.

So, I decided to take the next step and search for a Buddhist teacher. I was living in Indianapolis at the time, and a quick Google search led me to JDPSN (*Ji Do Poep Sa Nim*) Linc Rhodes and the Indianapolis Zen Center. The thing that struck me most about Linc when I first met him was how down to earth he was.

He wore sweatpants under his robes, and he liked to talk sports with me between classes. Once, he even gave me some advice on how to repair some body damage on my car. I had some strange ideas of what it meant to practice Zen in those days. I thought it entailed secret rituals and mystic powers at the higher levels. But Linc helped bring me back down to earth. He showed me that real Buddhism isn't separate from everyday life.

Our practice consisted of 108 prostrations followed by seated meditation and chanting. We also did work practice once a week on Saturdays, which involved cleaning up around the center, tending to the grounds, and assisting with carpentry projects. Afterward, Linc would feed everyone a vegetarian lunch and chat with us about our lives.

I should stop here and say that I was a terrible carpenter. The fact that Linc didn't ban me from the center after some of my screw-ups is a testament to just how accomplished he is as a Zen teacher. However, I learned a lot just from watching the way he handled unpleasant situations.

For example, there was one project we worked on where I was tasked with removing some old carpeting from the stairs, which led to the second floor of the center. I didn't know what I was doing, so I tried to make up for my lack of knowledge with enthusiasm as I went about my work. Unfortunately, I ended up doing a fair amount of damage to the hardwood under the carpet in the process.

When Linc came over to check my work, I knew immediately from the look on his face that I'd screwed up. In fact, I'm pretty sure he went through the entire spectrum of human emotion in about five seconds. I watched as the look of shock on his face was replaced with anger, sadness, and finally acceptance. Then he took a long, slow breath.

"This is it," I thought to myself. "I'm about to be excommunicated." But Linc didn't kick me out. Instead, he very calmly took the hammer and pry bar that I'd been using out of my hands and showed me the correct way to pull up the carpet. His demeanor was strained but calm. And when he finished giving me instructions, he looked up at me, smiled, and said, "There are many ways to do it, but some ways hurt less than others."

Those words changed my life forever. On the surface, he was speaking about carpentry work, but I also like to think that Linc was giving me a deeper, Buddhist lesson with that remark, kind of like how Mr. Miyagi teaches Daniel karate by making him wax cars. Essentially, Linc's remark was an excellent summation of the fourth noble truth that states, "The way to end desire is the Eightfold Path," and why it's so important to Buddhist practice.

The Eightfold Path is a framework that the Buddha created to help practitioners lead happier, more fulfilled lives. Naturally, these teachings are no guarantee that life will be a basket of roses, but they help us ensure that we don't make things worse than they need to be. The tenets of the Eightfold Path are:

**Right View** - We must work to see the world as it truly is, free from our preference of how it should be.

**Right Intention** - We must be committed to morality and ethical behavior in our dealings with others.

**Right Speech** - We must abstain from speech that is either untrue or divisive and use our words to improve the lives of ourselves and others.

**Right Action** - We must abstain from causing harm to ourselves and other sentient beings

**Right Livelihood** - We must earn a living in a way that doesn't cause harm to ourselves or other sentient beings, abstaining from the slave trade, prostitution, animal butchery, and the sale of intoxicants and poisons.

**Right Effort** - We must abstain from giving in to unwholesome mind-states (e.g., greed, anger, and ignorance) while simultaneously working to arouse wholesome mind-states (e.g., gratitude, faith, and compassion).

**Right Mindfulness** - We must learn about the nature of reality by contemplating our bodies, thoughts, emotions, and mental objects.

**Right Concentration -** We must practice meditation daily to free ourselves from negative mental impulses.

What I like about the tenets of the Eightfold Path is that they aren't a list of commandments. They're guidelines that practitioners can engage in conversation. We study them and try to implement each one to end suffering for ourselves and others. But it's up to us to decide how to do that. It's almost like Buddha said, "There are many ways to live, but this way hurts less than others."

I like to think that Linc was channeling that teaching when he showed me the correct way to pull up the carpet. Then again, maybe he just wanted me to stop screwing up the stairs.

**Lesson:** There are many ways to live. Choose the way that hurts the least.

## A Three-Pronged Approach to Buddhist Practice

The illiteracy rates in India were extremely high during the time that the Buddha was teaching. Most common people were busy with the daily struggle to survive, and they didn't have time to learn how to read and write. And even if they did, paper was a very rare commodity back then, so there probably wasn't much for them to read anyway.

As a result, when Buddha and his monastics went out each day to teach the Dharma, they did it as part of an oral tradition. The Buddha would sit and give talks to his disciples about Buddhism, and they memorized the teachings so that they could give them to others.

Naturally, this meant that the teachings needed to be easy to remember. So, Buddhism is a religion that's filled with many sub-groups and lists of teachings. We have the Four Noble Truths, the Noble Eightfold Path, the Four Dharma Seals, etc. And each list represents an easy-to-remember nugget of Buddhist knowledge.

Regarding the Noble Eightfold Path, the eight tenets are grouped into three separate categories, which represent a specific type of practice on the path. The categories and the tenets that fall under them are as follows:

> **Wisdom** - Right View and Right Intention

> **Morality** - Right Speech, Right Action, and Right Livelihood

> **Meditation** - Right Effort, Right Mindfulness, and Right Concentration

There is some debate regarding how Buddhist practitioners should approach the Noble Eightfold Path. Some schools teach that students should view it as a ladder, starting at the bottom with the wisdom practices and working their way up to the meditative ones.

This is a logical approach because once a person has a strong understanding of wisdom and morality, they'll have created the optimal environment for meditation, having removed many of the bad habits or misunderstandings that could be a hindrance to practice.

On the other hand, some Buddhist schools teach that students should focus their efforts on the meditative practices because the insight that one gains through meditation encompasses both morality and wisdom. That is to say, if one truly penetrates the great matter of life and death through meditation, then they won't need written precepts (part of Right View) to treat others with respect. They'll look at everyone they meet, see their own face, and act accordingly.

This is also a logical approach. After all, people don't need a doctor's note to tell them to wear gloves in the winter. They intuitively understand that their hands are part of their body. As a result, they put gloves on when it's cold without a second thought. Similarly, when one intuitively understands the interconnectedness of all living things, they'll care for other people in the same way that they care for their own hands. A rigorous meditation practice can provide this understanding.

Personally, I think it's a false dichotomy. The teachings were being delivered orally at the time of the Buddha, so he would have needed to be very efficient in his explanations of the Way. So, we can safely assume that he wouldn't have bothered teaching all of eight tenets of the path unless they were all equally important. A wise Buddhist practitioner incorporates them all into their training.

However, the order in which they are practiced will differ based on each student's temperament and understanding. For my part, meditation has always been the primary focus of my training. It took about two years of sitting on the cushion before things like the precepts or the sutras were more than just words on a page. However, now that I've progressed further, I study the sutras every day in addition to my meditation.

Of course, it may work differently for others, and that's perfectly fine. The key to remember is that every tenet of the Noble Eightfold path is necessary if we hope to attain nirvana and realize enlightenment. We should strive to incorporate them all into our training.

**Lesson:** Find a foothold on the Noble Eightfold path and use it to realize enlightenment!

## Zen and the Art of Playing Board Games

I grew up in a large family with five siblings and more cousins than I could handle. Family gatherings were always fun with lots of food, music, and stories about old times. When the kids were finally coming down off their sugar highs and worn out from chasing each other outside, it was common for us to end the night with a board game before everyone went home.

Depending on what game we chose, this usually resulted in some more laughs and good feelings. However, my heart always dropped if someone pulled out Monopoly. Sadly, that game seemed to bring out the evil in everyone's soul.

The rules of Monopoly are simple. Each player receives a game piece that represents them as they move around the board. The perimeter of the board contains squares with names like Park Place and Reading Railroad. Players roll dice to determine how many squares they can move on each turn, and then they're given different options based on where they land.

So, they may land on an open square and be allowed to buy that property. Or they may land on a square that's owned by another player. In that case, they'd be forced to pay rent. The last person standing when everyone else goes bankrupt is the winner.

The games always went on forever, to the point that all the children who were bright-eyed and bushy-tailed at the start of the game were cranky and tired by the end. Because so many of us wanted to play, we formed teams with two players using a single game piece. This led to endless arguments about whether specific properties should or shouldn't be purchased.

And to top it all off, alliances were formed between opposing players based on who did or didn't like each other on that day. Deals were made, hearts were broken, and an endless stream of tears were shed.

The game always ended badly, but for some reason, we kept playing. I don't know why. Maybe it was just a habit. Or maybe we honestly thought that things would go differently this time if we changed the teams up or played by a slightly different set of rules. Either way, we kept playing monopoly, and it kept ruining our night.

But something changed for me when I was 12. It was the Fourth of July, and we'd just come back from watching the fireworks display at a local park. All the kids were still wound up from the show, and there was no school the next day, so we had permission to stay up late.

My mom suggested that we play a game, and my little brother ran to our living room closet to pick one. He came back with Monopoly. "Do you want to play, Alex," he asked with a big smile on his face. Dread filled my heart as I thought about how the next two - three hours of my life were about to go. And then it occurred to me that I didn't have to play, I could say no.

I'm not sure why that never occurred to me before. I think part of me felt obligated to participate in every game and accept every invitation as a child. I thought people wouldn't like me if I didn't. But in that moment, I was 12 years old, practically a man in my mind. And my pre-teen brain wanted to assert itself.

"No," I said, "I'm tired; I'm going to bed." Fear gripped my heart for a moment after I spoke. I was worried that I'd hurt his feelings. But he just shrugged, dumped the box's contents at his feet unceremoniously, and started setting up the pieces. Crisis averted, I quickly said goodnight to everyone else in my family and went upstairs to my room.

Over time, this became my modus operandi whenever the question of board games came up. I'd wait to see what we were playing, and if the game was Monopoly, I'd find some excuse (bedtime, homework, stomachache, etc.) not to play. As a result, I spent many evenings alone in my room with my nose buried in a book, thankful that I wasn't part of the chaos that was taking place in the living room.

Eventually, my parents caught on to what I was doing, and I was forced to explain my strong dislike of Monopoly. They were understanding. But they didn't like the fact that I was isolating myself in my room. So, the next time my siblings wanted to play Monopoly, everyone talked, and we agreed to the following caveats:

1. The game would only last 30 minutes. After that, we'd count our money, and whoever had the most would win.
2. No alliances could be formed against other players

3. No one could take money from the bank except the banker (my mom), and she would be the referee if there was disagreement around the rules.

With the new rules in place, the game was completely different. By the time we finished everyone was still smiling, no one cried, and my neck didn't hurt from being hunched over the board for hours.

"Can we play again?" my little sister asked. She'd won the game and was hoping to double down on her victory. Both of my parents looked at me out of the corner of their eyes. "Yeah, I'll play," I said as I started putting the board back together, "same rules as before."

When we discuss the wisdom teachings of the Noble Eightfold Path, we're essentially talking about learning to practice Right View, which helps us see the problem of suffering in the world and find solutions to that problem — then practicing right intention to implement those solutions.

Of course, I didn't think of it this way when I was 12, but that's essentially what happened with the Monopoly game. I saw that the way that we were playing the game was a source of suffering, not happiness for my family and me. I found a good initial solution, which involved simply refusing to play. And later I worked with my family to come up with another solution, which involved playing the game with slightly different rules.

This is all very simple on the surface, but it can be difficult to put into practice. When our minds cloud with desire, we're unable to see the consequences of our actions. Often, we end up clinging to the very things that hurt us because we think they'll bring us happiness.

That's one of the reasons why it's not useful to use shame or guilt tactics when trying to get people to change their behavior. Even if someone knows intellectually that an action is morally wrong or unhealthy, they won't change their behavior unless they can see the suffering that is caused by it and develop a strong resolve to end that suffering.

That's why the First Noble Truth states unequivocally, "Life is suffering." It is an attempt by Buddha to help us develop Right View and a clear understanding of our existential problem. Once we have a clear understanding and acceptance of that statement, then it begs the following questions:

1. Where does life's suffering come from?
2. What can I do about it?
3. How do I enact the necessary changes to end suffering?

These questions are answered by the second, third, and fourth noble truths, which state, "Suffering is caused by desire" and "The way to end suffering is to end desire," and "The way to end desire is the Noble Eightfold Path." So, one would be correct in stating that a person who has developed Right View has developed a clear understanding and appreciation of the Four Noble Truths.

However, it is important to note that people have many desires that cause suffering for themselves and others. So, the Buddhist path is not a straight line. Rather, it is a circle, and practitioners will have to walk the path many times with various desires throughout their lifetime.

For example, it's possible for someone to have a clear understanding that lying is a source of suffering but be heavily involved in gambling. So, that same person could be honest and upright in dealings with family and friends but carry huge amounts of debt and be unable to pay bills because they constantly lose money at the casino.

Or someone could completely abstain from drinking alcohol because they clearly understand the suffering that comes from abusing intoxicants but cheat on their spouse with multiple sexual partners.

In both cases, the person in question has successfully walked the path in one area of their life (e.g., lying and drinking), but they have failed to walk it in a different area of their life (e.g., gambling and sex). For this reason, Right View requires us to examine our lives both at the aggregate level and at the minute level, examining each of our desires and the suffering that is generated by them.

Another part of Right View is developing a good understanding of karma. Karma is the chain of cause and effect that plays out as a result of our actions. Everything we do generates karma. Sometimes we can see the karmic effects of our actions, and sometimes we can't, but the effects are always there.

When I was a child playing Monopoly, I was able to see the karmic chain of events that was leading to suffering for myself and others. At first my understanding was very simple. I just knew that every time we played Monopoly, it ended with everyone getting mad at each other. So, I developed a simple solution in renunciation; I didn't play the game anymore.

Later, my understanding changed. After talking with my parents, I realized that the suffering was tied more closely to the way that we played the game, not the game itself.

When we worked together as a family to come up with better rules for the game, we eliminated many of the negative karmic effects.

A clear understanding of karma is important because that's what allows us to draw straight lines between our actions and their consequences, our desire, and our suffering. Once we have that, it becomes much easier to create positive karma that makes life happier and more peaceful for ourselves and others.

Once we have Right View, we'll no longer make choices based on greed, anger, and ignorance. Instead, we'll strive to do things from a place of peace and equanimity.

Again, this sounds simplistic, but it's not. When the mind is filled with desire, it becomes difficult to see the consequences of our actions. As a result, we can create hardship in the world without meaning too. That's why the wisdom, morality, and meditative practices of the Eightfold Path are so closely related. They create karmic chains of events that help to end suffering.

For example, with the Monopoly game 12-year old me practiced Right View, and Right Intention when I realized that the game was causing suffering, and I resolved to stop it. That led to Right Mindfulness when my parents and I investigated our bodies, speech, and minds to determine how we were causing that suffering. This mindfulness practice led to us engaging in Right Action by changing the rules so that less pain and misery would occur.

As Buddhists, we go through similar cycles many times each day. When we are at work, school, or with our families, we use Right View and Right Intention to see the suffering of the world and resolve to fix it if we are able. This naturally leads us to one of the meditative or morality teachings, which in turn reinforces our Right View and Right Intention.

This endless cycle is why a wheel symbolizes Buddhism with eight spokes on it. Each spoke represents a tenet of the Noble Eightfold Path. Right View and Right Intention help us turn this "wheel of Dharma," and each time it spins life becomes more peaceful for the people around us and us.

**Lesson:** Life is a board game; spin the Dharma wheel!


## A Land of Rivers and Trees

Some people chafe at the idea of moral teachings. Perhaps they don't like the idea of being told what to do, or maybe they have been harmed previously by people who used corrupt rules to their advantage. In either case, it is understandable that such a person distrusts rules and regulations.

However, the importance of moral teachings as they relate to Buddhism cannot be overstated. The Buddha laid out an extensive code of conduct in the Vinaya Suttas that detailed how monastics were expected to behave in daily life. He did this to ensure that even highly unrealized Buddhists who were new to the practice could set a good example for the lay community and behave in a way that helped the Sangha remain cohesive.

For lay practitioners, it is also necessary to set a good example for others and behave in a way that helps society remain cohesive. So, while lay people may not abide by all

277 precepts that were laid out for male monastics or the 311 precepts that were laid out for female monastics, they should still abide by the moral tenets of the Noble Eightfold Path, which are Right Speech, Right Action, and Right Livelihood.

In my own life, I see these tenets less as rules that I'm forced to follow and more like guideposts that help keep me on the path. They provide a measuring stick that I can use to ensure that my speech, action, and livelihood are in keeping with the Dharma.

To put it another way, let's imagine that we travel to a faraway land. And when we get there, we find a massive forest with fruit trees of every variety. Also, in the middle of that forest, there is a lake, which spouts rivers in every direction. So, we're in a place with more food than we could ever eat, and more water than we could ever drink.

But what if only some of the rivers that came from the lake had clean water, and the others were poisonous? Moreover, what if only some of the fruit trees were good to eat from, and the others were poisonous? That would be a problem. We'd have to wander the land with no idea what to eat or drink! Of course, we could figure it out through trial and error. But we'd probably make some mistakes along the way that resulted in us getting sick or possibly dying.

Finally, let's imagine that in our travels we discover a set of books that give detailed descriptions of the trees and rivers in our new country. The people who wrote the books lived in this land before us, and while they are incomplete in places due to changes that have occurred since those people died, they provide a good starting point in figuring out where to safely get food and water.

If we lived in this land, and we found these books, wouldn't it be foolish not to use them? That's precisely the situation we live in now as Dharma practitioners. The modern world provides a near-infinite amount of options in terms of how we want to live our lives. As a result, it can be difficult to determine what moral code we should live by, or how we can respond in various situations.

The moral teachings that we find in the Buddhist sutras represent the thoughts and experiences of men and women who've "been there, done that" regarding many of the situations that we find ourselves in. Thus, the sutras are the embodiment of 2,600 years of life experience that we can refer to in times of confusion.

Of course, we can't use them without inserting our own ideas and interpretations. We're not monastics living in the time of the Buddha, and it would be unwise to live as if we were. However, the moral tenets of the Noble Eightfold Path provide a solid framework for us to use. More than that, they help us create the causes for positive karma to manifest in our lives.

But before we can understand how that works, we need to clear up a common misconception. That is to say: people often assume that good people only have good things happen to them because of their karma. And bad people only have bad things happen to them because of their karma. But that's not always correct.

Our karma doesn't exist in a vacuum. It intersects with the karma of the people, places, and things around us, and this can lead to unexpected results. For example, if we throw a ball up into the air, then we've created a cause, and the expected karmic effect is that it will fall back down to the ground. But it's also possible that an eagle will swoop down from the sky, grab the ball in mid-air, and carry it away!

In this example, the eagle's karma intersected with our own and created an unexpected result. Now if we expand our view to imagine the infinite number of causes and effects that are being created by every living being on earth, it becomes easy to see why karma doesn't always play out as we expect.

Sometimes people commit crimes, and they go to jail immediately. Other times, they may escape detection for many years. Sometimes people do the right thing, and their life immediately improves. Other times, it may take several years of trying. But that doesn't mean that we can do whatever we want.

After all, while it's true that an eagle may swoop down and catch the ball in mid-air, the most likely result is that it falls back to the ground. And when it does, we better be there to catch it before it hits someone in the head! Similarly, while we can never know for certain what the effects of our actions will be, we can certainly predict what is most likely to cause positive effects and act accordingly.

I like to think of it in terms of planting seeds. For example, let's say that we're still living in our undiscovered country. But we've grown tired of wandering the wilderness, and we want to start an orchard. So, we gather seeds from the trees that bear healthy, non-poisonous fruit, and we clear a plot of land.

First, we fertilize the soil. Next, we till the soil, plant our seeds, and build irrigation to ensure that the fruit trees have plenty of water. We work hard to do everything correctly, but at a certain point, it's out of our hands. Some of the seeds will grow, and some of them won't. We don't have any control over that. However, since we only planted seeds from trees that are good to eat from, the chances of poisonous fruit appearing in our orchard are slim.

Furthermore, since we fertilized the soil and provided irrigation, we've created the causes for lots of the seeds to turn into healthy, fruit-bearing trees. We've created the karmic effects for good things to come into our lives.

The moral tenets of the Noble Eightfold Path work in the same way. Each time we practice Right Speech, Right Action, and Right Livelihood we plant the karmic seeds for good things to happen both to ourselves and others. Furthermore, when we fertilize the soil and provide irrigation by also practicing other tenets like Right Intention and Right Mindfulness, we increase the chances of those seeds growing into big beautiful trees.

Some of those trees will grow in our lifetime. Some of them will grow much later and benefit the people who come after us. But if we keep planting seeds, some of them will grow. We just need to have faith and be determined never to stop trying.

**Lesson:** Plant the seeds for good things to happen.

# Passing Through the Fence

Imagine for a moment that we are trapped at the bottom of a great chasm. For a long time, we don't realize our predicament, and we wander in the darkness like wild animals, struggling through muck and grime. One day, a ray of light from far away flashes in our eyes, and our thinking changes.

Suddenly, we realize that we're at the bottom of an enormous hole, and we decide that we don't want to be here anymore. The more we think about it, the more we dislike being down here, covered in filth, and we begin working to find a way out. Finally, after a good deal of searching, we find a ladder with three rungs on it.

Carefully, we jump up and grab the bottom rung of the ladder. We pull ourselves up and begin reaching for the next rung on the ladder, but at the last moment, we slip and fall back into the bottom of the hole! Undeterred, we reach for the bottom rung of the ladder and pull ourselves up again.

It takes a few tries, but eventually, we climb up the ladder, and we get out of the chasm. But our journey isn't finished yet. There is a giant fence around the hole we just came out of, and there are no ladders in sight. However, there is enough room between the fence and the chasm that we can sit and rest comfortably.

We spend a few moments just taking it all in. Our situation is much better than it was in the chasm. There is fresh air and sunshine up here. For the first time, we feel like we can think clearly, and our mind feels calm and peaceful. We look through the fence, and on the other side, we see a huge mountain of treasure! There are gold coins, gemstones, and pearls piled as high as the eye can see. Even better, there is a sign in front of the treasure with our names on it! The treasure belongs to us. Now, if only we could get past this fence.

When our minds are clouded by greed, anger, and ignorance, it is like being at the bottom of a dark hole. We chase after sensual desires with no thought of the consequences, blind to the inherent enlightenment that lies within us. Thankfully, the Noble Eightfold Path provides a method for climbing out of the darkness.

In the above story, the light that flashed in our eyes was the light of Dharma shining through the millennia via Buddha's teachings. The filth that we wallowed through was the negative karma that we created through our actions. When we were able to see the crisis that we were experiencing, that was Right View, and it was Right Intention that helped us gain the resolve to escape.

The three rungs of the ladder represented Right Speech, Right Action, and Right Livelihood, the moral tenets that help pull us out of the darkness created by greed, anger, and ignorance. The resting place at the top of the chasm was nirvana, the state of peacefulness created when our minds aren't clouded by desire.

When we got there, we saw a giant treasure with our names on it. That treasure was our inherent enlightenment. Now, it's important to note that the treasure was always there. We were/are already enlightened; however, we didn't realize that fact until we climbed out of the hole. That's why I always tell students that we attain nirvana, but we realize enlightenment.

Because we don't naturally have nirvana (a peaceful mind free of greed, anger, and ignorance), but that is something that we can work toward and attain through effort. However, we can't attain enlightenment because it's something that we already possess. Rather, we must calm our minds enough that we can see our enlightenment and manifest it in daily life.

But before we can do that we have to get through the fence. The fence represents the limits of intellectual thought on the spiritual path. Our brains can certainly move us along the path, and moral actions can give us a glimmer of our enlightened natures. But to fully embody our enlightenment, we must experience it directly.

This is where the meditative tenets of the Noble Eightfold Path come into play. The practices of Right Effort, Right Mindfulness, and Right Concentration help us to study the mind, sit with our thoughts, and temporarily let go of our intellectual ways of thinking. This allows us to experience our enlightened natures more fully, which results in us engaging in moral/enlightened actions in daily life.

Thus, the practice is not a straight line. It's a circle. Enlightened action creates the necessary conditions for enlightened experience, which then results in us performing more enlightened action. It's an endless cycle. That's why when Buddhists walk the path, we walk it for a lifetime.

That's also why when the Buddha realized his own enlightenment under the Bodhi tree, his response was to keep practicing and teaching for the next 45 years until his death. Even for the "awakened one," there was always one more step to go, and one more fence to push through.

**Lesson:** You're almost there; don't quit!

# Right View

# Straight-Edge Buddhism

The straight-edge movement started as part of the hardcore punk music scene in the early '80s. At that time, drugs and alcohol were thought by many to be ruining the scene, and punks began to abstain from intoxicants in response.

Some adherents went so far as to abstain from promiscuous sex and eating meat as well. This was a response to the consumerist ideologies and rampant conformity that punks stood against.

I was born a little too late to get involved in the punk scene, but I spent my early 20s as a raver, so I can relate to a lot of the complaints that punks had regarding the mix of drugs, alcohol, and music.

I used to go to parties and dance until my whole body was sore, mesmerized by all of the glow-sticking and "four to the floor" beats. But it was always a bit of downer when I went with people who only wanted to score drugs and get high in the chill room. The breaking point came when I watched a close friend overdose. She survived, but I was done with raves after that.

Lately, I've been thinking about the straight-edge movement and how it relates to Buddhism. At its core, the straight-edge movement is all about renunciation, which is entirely in keeping with Buddhist practice. In fact, one could argue that Buddha was straight edge before it was cool. (See what I did there?)

This has been on my mind a lot lately because it seems like drugs and alcohol are becoming increasingly more accepted in Buddhist circles. In fact, some practitioners argue that drugs are an important part of the awakening process.

I have no interest in arguing with these people. But I'd like to present an alternative view for Buddhist practitioners who aren't monastics. What if we had a Straight-Edge Buddhist movement? What if we abstained from drugs, alcohol, and promiscuous sex to further our practice? Could renunciation help us end suffering for ourselves and others?

Honestly, it's not a radical idea. When Mahayana Buddhists take the five lay precepts, they promise to refrain from several things. We'd just need to be stricter in our approach in the following ways:

**To refrain from killing:** This is generally understood as refraining from taking human life. But one could take it a step farther by being vegetarian/vegan or doing Meatless Mondays.

**To refrain from stealing:** As straight-edge Buddhists, could we do one better and strive to practice generosity (the opposite of stealing) in our daily lives?

**To refrain from lying/gossiping:** What if we went further than simply not lying and actively worked to give people compliments throughout the day?

**To refrain from sexual misconduct:** Most people read this as not engaging in acts of rape or incest. That certainly makes sense, but could we expand that to include abstaining from sex outside of committed relationships and practicing affirmative consent.

**To refrain from abusing intoxicants:** For Buddhists who are interested in a straight-edge lifestyle, I'd suggest that this would involve not drinking alcohol and abstaining from drugs that aren't prescribed by a doctor.

I like the idea of Straight-Edge Buddhism because it allows lay practitioners to move closer to the orthodox teachings of Buddhism while still living the life of a householder.

Additionally, it provides a guidepost for enlightened behavior, which is helpful on days when we aren't feeling enlightened. In this way, we can protect our "scene" and refrain from harmful activities just like the punks did all those years ago.

**Lesson:** The precepts are a springboard from which our spiritual practice can grow.

## How to Say "I love you" in Buddhism

In conventional society the relationship between emotion and action is simple. We become aware of something in our environment, it causes an emotional response, and we act accordingly. So, if a man sees someone on the street that he likes, that person will elicit positive emotions, resulting in the man behaving positively. He might smile or shout a greeting in response.

However, if that same man sees someone on the street that he dislikes, that person will elicit negative emotions, resulting in the man behaving negatively. He might look away or shout an insult in response. The formula for this chain of events is awareness + emotion = action.

Of course, this places the impetus on the people and things around us to make us feel good. In other words, if someone wants us to be nice, then they must be nice to us first. Similarly, if we want to be happy, we need to surround ourselves with people and things that make us happy. Anything that does otherwise is discarded.

That's all well and good, but we take a different approach to life in Buddhism. Instead of allowing our emotions to drive our actions, we engage in certain actions in the hope that they'll create certain feelings within us.

For example, if a student is behaving arrogantly, a Buddhist teacher might instruct them to do 1,000 prostrations before the altar. The act of bowing is one of humility. So, doing 1,000 prostrations will teach the student to be humble. Similarly, if a student is feeling anger toward a family member, the teacher might instruct them to give that person a gift. The act of gift-giving is one of friendship so that this action will replace the feeling of anger in the student with one of friendliness. The formula for this chain of events is awareness + action = emotion.

One way to understand this is to look at the way we express love in Buddhism. The first part of the equation is *Karuna*, which is a Pali word that means "compassionate-action." It's important to note, however, that the practice of Karuna is not concerned with the emotional feeling of compassion, which normally involves a sense of pity or sadness. Rather, it's directed toward actions that alleviate suffering.

The second half of the equation is *Metta*, which is Pali for "Loving-kindness." In this case, the focus is not on the feeling of affection that we normally associate with kindness. Rather, it's on the expression of kindness through loving-actions. That is to say, it encourages actions that create feelings of goodwill and joy.

When one develops right view and sees the suffering that exists in the world, the natural response is one of Karuna and Metta. Reflexively, we work to make life more peaceful for ourselves and others in the same way that we reflexively pull our hand from a hot stove.

But it's difficult to see the world clearly when the mind is clouded with desire. As a result, we must train ourselves to perform Karuna and Metta when we may not have the desire to do so. That's why ritual is an important part of Buddhist practice.

The amount of ceremony that takes place within a temple may seem strange to an outsider, but it all has a purpose. Bowing teaches humility, giving offerings of food and incense teaches Metta, and cleaning the meditation hall teaches Karuna. Each part of the ritual is designed to cultivate a healthy, life-affirming mind state within us. Awareness + Action = Emotion.

Thus, love isn't a noun in Buddhism; it's a verb. It's not something we feel, so much as it's something we do. And each moment of our life can be an expression of that love because the goal of Buddhist love is to relieve suffering (Karuna) and create joy (Metta) for ourselves and others.

Each time we practice Buddhist ritual, we say, "I love you." Each time we prepare food for our families or smile at a co-worker, we say, "I love you." And each time we engage in action that creates benefit, not harm, for ourselves and others, we say, "I love you," to the world.

But that's not the end of the story. Because Right View also helps us see how much the world loves us. The electricity that heats our home is an "I love you" from power plant workers far away. The food that sits on shelves in the grocery store is an "I love you" from farmers that we'll never meet. And the existence of countless Buddhist books, articles, and sutras that help us in our practice is an "I love you" that goes back to the Buddha himself.

So, Right View helps us see the suffering of the world. But it also helps us see the love in it. And once we see all the kindness and generosity that life gives us each day, our response is automatic. We wake up each morning, and find ways to say, "I love you, too."

**Lesson:** Wake up and spread the love.

## Cedar Siding and Tiny Houses

In the fall of 2014, I left corporate America. All the meditation that I'd been doing for the last two years had left me feeling mentally raw, and I was sensitive to the politics, backstabbing, and overall callousness that I witnessed in conference rooms each day.

More than that, I was tired of feeling like a faceless cog in the machine of a business enterprise. I think I'd always felt this way to some extent, but my desire for security and material possessions had kept me showing up to work despite that. I'd adopted a "work hard, play hard" approach, which allowed me to justify doing unsatisfying work by focusing on the sensual pleasures that I could purchase with my paycheck.

"Focus on the money," had become my mantra over the years, and that worked fine if the driving forces in my life were greed and anger. But as Buddhism started to change my mindset, it also changed the way I viewed both the world and the way I earned a living. At the end of each day, I found myself wondering, "What am I doing this for," and more importantly, "Who am I doing this for?"

The frustration that I was feeling at the time can best be described in the language of Martin Buber, a theologian who categorized human relationships as either I – It or I – Thou. The I - It relationship is utilitarian. This relationship involves human beings living as automatons who only exist for the benefit of others. So, the plumber, the waiter, the office worker, etc. all lack value outside of the profit they can generate for other, more powerful people.

On the other hand, the I – Thou relationship is holistic, placing value on the entire person. So, each person has a value that is incalculable based on their relationship to the divine. And since we're all children of the divine, we interact with each other from the viewpoint of wholeness. *Who* you are is much more important than *what* you can do. In the parlance of Martin Buber, I was tired of feeling like an It. And I wanted to live in a way that allowed me to both see and be seen through the lens of an I – Thou relationship.[10]

Inspired by documentaries like *Amongst White Clouds* that detailed the lives of Zen monks who had successfully separated themselves from conventional society to focus on Buddhist practice, I wanted to get closer to nature.[11] But I wasn't sure how to do that. I had student loans that needed to be paid and a family that wouldn't approve of me disappearing into the forest.

I found a solution when I learned about sustainable farming apprenticeships. Simply put, sustainable farming is an agricultural philosophy that emphasizes doing the least amount of damage to the environment as possible while maximizing the amount of food that's grown. The use of chemical pesticides, herbicides, and fertilizers are avoided, replaced by armies of (largely) unpaid volunteers who pull weeds by hands, utilize permaculture techniques to limit pests naturally, and shovel endless amounts of compost into the fields.

Due to the low-tech, hands-on approach that sustainable farming operations require, the farm owners often live in community with their apprentices. Meals and living areas are shared, the farm owners often labor side-by-side with the workers, and a larger focus is (usually) placed on building relationships within the group.

The living arrangements differ from one farm to the next, but the basic premise is that apprentices agree to give the farm owner a certain number of hours of free labor in exchange for food and shelter. Generally, there is also an understanding that the apprentice will have the chance to learn about the business of farming through classes and the experiential learning that comes with repairing fences, caring for animals, working in the fields.

My plan was simple. I'd do a couple of unpaid apprenticeships to build up my sustainable farming resume in the same way that I'd built up my corporate one. Then I'd work my way into seasonal, paid jobs. My expenses would be low enough living off the land that what little money I made could all go to paying my phone bill and student loans. My lifestyle would be different than the Zen hermits that I idolized, but I'd still spend my days in nature, doing manual labor and studying Buddhism in my free time.

The only downside of this plan was that I'd no longer be able to practice at the Indianapolis Zen Center. I'd spent a year training with JDPSN (*Ji Do Poep Sa Nim*) Linc Rhodes, the guiding teacher of the center, and learning from his example. I sat my first retreats with him. He was my first preceptor, and the vegetarian meals that Linc served during retreats and after work practice influenced my decision to eat a plant-based diet. But there was no getting around it; I'd have to walk the path alone for a while.

He didn't say it, but I could tell Linc was concerned when I told him my plans. And who wouldn't be worried when a student says that they are quitting their job to work for free on someone else's farm. But Linc had never been one to tell other people what to do. Even when I wanted him to give me clear direction, he always forced me to figure things out for myself. He was a great teacher in that way. So, I sat a final two-day retreat with him, and then we parted ways as friends.

I ended up landing a five-month natural building apprenticeship on a farm in Indiana. The farm owner was named Robert. He was having an off-the-grid tiny house built on the property, and he needed an extra set of hands to get it finished by spring. So, I stripped down my possessions to what could fit into a large military-issued duffle bag and asked a friend to drive me to the property.

The farm itself looked like something out of a brochure. It sat on 75 acres, and it was surrounded by forest. There was a large warehouse that had been converted into a community center. It housed a kitchen, dining area, and a designated space for yoga and meditation. One of the requirements of the apprenticeship was that each of us took turns preparing breakfast, lunch, and dinner for the other community members. I'm proud to say that I spent many hours in that kitchen experimenting with different dishes. And I learned to make fantastic lentils and beans soup as a result.

There was an outdoor kitchen, complete with a rocket stove — several off-the-grid cabins, and three large greenhouses that grew a variety of leafy green vegetables. Additionally, there were open areas with pasture-raised pigs, chickens, and cows.

I felt strange helping to care for animals that I knew were being raised for slaughter. But I took solace in the fact that each animal that came from there was one less that came from a factory farm. I also had an agreement with Robert that I wouldn't have to participate in the slaughter of the animals under my care. It was an imperfect solution, but I've learned that life rarely gives us perfect ones.

There were seven apprentices including myself. Five were assigned to farming duties, which meant that they would be responsible for animal care, attending farmers markets, and harvesting plants from the fields and greenhouses. I was on the building crew with Jack, the building leader, and another apprentice named Mark.

Mark was tall and thin with curly black hair and olive-colored skin. His story was similar to mine in that he graduated from college, got a job as an accountant, and quickly realized that there was no way he could work in an office for the rest of his life.

So, he decided to walk a different path that included venturing to South America to study Shamanism and teaching English in Vietnam for two years. Mark and I spent endless hours down at the building site discussing Shamanism, Buddhism, and the evils of corporate America.

In contrast, Jack was short and heavyset. He had long yellowish, white hair that he kept pulled back in a ponytail. He was around 60 years old, a bona fide hippie who'd lived through the sexual revolution, the Cold War, and the civil rights movement. Jack was a certified, professional carpenter who'd built an off-the-grid holistic healing center in Canada before problems with his visa forced him to return to the states.

The tiny house had a unique design that had been created by Jack during his time in Canada. It had a hexagonal footprint as opposed to the typical square/rectangle shape of a traditional house. So, the walls were formed using interlocking triangles, a shape that gives the greatest amount of structural integrity with the least amount of materials.

The apprentices who had come before us had done a fair amount of work on the structure, but there was still a lot to do before the house could be considered livable. A door frame and new door needed to be installed, a floor and wood stove needed to be added to the interior, and insulation needed to be installed to protect from the cold Indiana winters.

Each morning, Jack would meet with Mark and me to go over our work assignments for the day. And then he'd send us down to the work site while he did miscellaneous maintenance tasks around the farm. Mark had grown up doing maintenance work in his uncle's apartment complex, and we quickly decided that he was the superior carpenter. So, he handled the work that required an artist's touch while I assisted by cutting wood, digging holes, and carrying heavy things when needed.

Of all the work that we did on the tiny house, my least favorite part was putting siding on the outside of it. Naturally, that was also the task that took the longest for us to complete. On our third day at the farm, Mark and I went on a trip with Robert where we picked up cedar wood from an Amish sawmill. The slabs came from the cedar trees that were cut into 2 x 4s, leaving rounded slabs that couldn't be used in traditional building projects. However, given the waterproof nature of cedar, the slabs were perfect for our building project.

The only problem was that since the walls of the tiny house were made of interlocking triangles that started wide at one end and narrowed to a point at the other, we couldn't just cut each slab to a designated length and then nail it on the wall.

We had to measure each one, cut it to length with a circular saw, and then cut the ends of each slab at an angle so it wouldn't overlap with the other sections. It took about three days of trial and error for Mark and me to work out a system that played to both of our strengths.

Mark would stand on the ladder and measure how long the cedar slab needed to be. Then I would go digging through the woodpile until I found something that looked promising, walk it over to our workbench, and cut it to length. Next, I'd climb up on a second ladder next to Mark, and we'd hold the slab up against the triangle section of the wall, using pencils to mark the angle that needed to be cut on either side.

After that, I'd climb down off the ladder, go back to the workbench, and cut the appropriate angle in each side of the slab. Finally, I'd climb back up the ladder, hold the slab, and we'd use a nail gun to attach it to the wall.

The most difficult part was the repetition. Mark and I must have gone through the same chain of events about 10,000 times before the siding was finished. Also, attention to detail was extremely important. If I cut the wrong angles in the wood, the slab wouldn't fit correctly on that section of the wall. We'd have to discard it and start over again with a new piece. Additionally, each slab had to overlap with the one beneath it to keep water from getting in between them and damaging the interior wall.

It didn't happen often, but there were a few times when Jack came down to inspect our work, decided that it wasn't up to par, and made us redo an entire day's worth of work. Those days were difficult. But if we started to grumble, he'd remind us that someone would be living there when we finished, and we owed it to them to do a good job.

This is also true of Buddhist practice. A diligent student can learn the necessary forms and major tenets of Buddhism in a short amount of time. However, it takes a lifetime of repeating those forms and studying those tenets to penetrate the teachings fully. This can be hard for Westerners to understand because we live in a fast-paced, I-want-it-now culture. But Buddhism is a lot like putting cedar siding on a house. There are no shortcuts. We learn how to practice correctly, and then we continue to practice 10,000 times until our "house" is complete.

Occasionally, our teacher may give us instructions that we dislike, telling us that we need to change what we're doing. But we're the ones who benefit from practicing correctly. And we're the ones who suffer if we practice incorrectly. Thus, we owe it to ourselves to do a good job and pay attention to the details.

This is true in a Buddhist temple, but it's also true in daily life. As humans, our existence is made up of small, seemingly insignificant acts that add up over time. Right View allows us to see the importance of these small acts and develop the discipline to do them correctly over and over again.

For example, if we forget to wash the dishes before going to bed one time, it's not a big deal. But if we forget to wash dishes for an entire week, we'll have a hard time finding dishes to eat our dinner!

So, we have a paradox where washing the dishes one time is seemingly unimportant. But washing them 10,000 times (consistently, every day) is important because that repetition ensures that we always have plates and silverware at our disposal. But we can't wash the dishes 10,000 times unless we start by washing them once. A single action done correctly and repeatedly makes all the difference in our lives.

Another example might be our interactions with other people. Smiling and showing kindness to a difficult coworker or a challenging relative probably won't pay dividends if we only do it once. However, if we do it consistently in the same way that Mark and I placed the slabs of cedar siding on the house, then eventually things will shift in a positive direction. It just takes time.

And as our Right View expands, we realize that this teaching applies to every facet of our life. Whether it's feeding the dog, saying, "I love you," to a family member, or sitting in meditation, doing it correctly one time probably won't change the world. However, doing it consistently and correctly 10,000 times will make our life into a waterproof, cedar-sided house that we'll be happy to call home.

**Lesson:** If it's worth doing once, it's worth doing 10,000 times.

## Politics and the Space Between Words

I've always had a healthy respect for the power of words. It started when I was a child, growing up with books as my only friends. I loved sitting in my room for hours and letting the written word take me to places all over the universe.

When I was younger, it was Ernest Hemingway's *Old Man and The Sea* that taught me about manhood, and Jack London's *Call of The Wild* that made me love the natural world.

As I got older, Rudyard Kipling's *The Jungle Book* taught me about loyalty, and Madeleine L'Engle's *A Wrinkle in Time* showed me the power of faith. I like to think of these books as my first Dharma teachers.

In college, my love of words turned into a love of debate. I joined my school's parliamentary debate team, and it was terrific fun! If your opponent said something you disagreed with, you could loudly yell, "For shame!" and if you wanted to support your debate partner in their arguments, you could shout, "Here, here!" to help them emphasize a point.

We debated in teams of two with one team being the government and the other team being the opposition. And there was a single moderator or judge who would both provide the debate topic and decide the winner. It was the government's job to flesh out the debate topic, define key terms, and make a case, which the opposition would attempt to refute. The first round was critical because whoever controlled the definitions of the keywords controlled the debate.

For example, if the debate topic was "What's good for the goose is good for the gander," the government might choose to take that statement as a metaphor, defining "goose" as a corporation and "gander" as the employee and then defining those terms in a way that would strengthen their argument.

Naturally, the opposition would respond by coming up with their own definitions, which weakened the government's argument while simultaneously making their argument stronger. As a result, I spent a small amount of time in college discussing actual debate topics and a whole lot of time trying to pin down the exact meaning of words.

Whoever came up with definitions that the judge liked best would inevitably be the winner. It was through my experiences on the debate team that I learned something mind-blowing. Words don't mean anything.

There is no final, all-encompassing definition that everyone abides by for words like good, bad, or balloon. Even if you check the dictionary, you find words being used to define other words, and if you read long enough, you inevitably wind up back at the word you're trying to define.

Language is nothing more than a circular logic algorithm, a nonsensical mess of symbols and sounds that we use to describe an existence that we can never truly understand. But knowing that doesn't keep me from sitting down at my laptop every night, writing words, and loving every minute of it. After all, language is an illusion, but that doesn't stop it from being real.

I've been thinking about this lately as it relates to our national discourse. There are a lot of words being thrown around these days like gun control, immigration, protests, etc. People are attached to these words, so much so that they say and do hurtful things to one another.

It's sad, but I suppose it can't be helped. For people to agree on anything they first must agree on the meaning of the words they're using. And most people don't know what they're saying. Sure, they may have strong feelings about a topic. But it's my experience that if I ask for a clear, concise definition of terms that will hold up in a parliamentary debate, they've got nothing.

This can be difficult to reconcile on the surface. How can words cause so much suffering if they have no inherent existence of their own, if we can't even explain what they mean? Buddha explained this dichotomy when he discussed the Two Truths Doctrine. The teaching states that both absolute reality (words are an illusion) and conventional reality (words are real and true) exist simultaneously. Furthermore, if we practice Right View regarding these apparent opposites, then our confusion will disappear. [12]

I like to think of the Two Truths Doctrine in terms of a child who just watched a scary movie. If we look at the situation through the lens of the absolute, the movie isn't real, there are no monsters under the bed, and there is nothing to fear. However, if we look at the same situation through the lens of conventional reality, we still have a scared child standing in front of us who needs to be comforted.

Both things are true at the same time. However, Right View allows us to see and appreciate the suffering of the child without being scared ourselves because we also see the bigger picture. Unfortunately, it doesn't seem like people can see the big picture anymore. They're so caught up in words and political movements that they can't access the peacefulness of the absolute. And they do terrible things to each other as a result.

But we can't ignore political debate completely. Each of us has a civic duty to be informed about the issues that affect us. It might be true that words and the larger institutions that are built upon them aren't real, but the suffering that they can cause certainly is.

I try to take a "middle way" by forming my own opinions about various subjects, but not worrying too much if other people agree with me. I've chosen to hang up my debating boots. I have my beliefs, and I strive to live by them, but I've stopped using words to try and make others behave as I think they should.

Instead, I choose to live in the space between words, the space before thoughts and aversion muddy the waters of life. It's easy to do. I just sit on my cushion, close my eyes, and breathe.

As I meditate, I leave my attachments and definitions behind, finding myself in a place of stillness, a place that only exists between the last word of a sentence… and the period.

**Lesson:** Use your words, but remember the peaceful place in between them

# Barking Buddhas

I have a confession to make. I'm not a dog person. It's not that I dislike dogs; quite the opposite. I grew up with them, and I think the world would be a better place if people were more dog-like. But dogs require a lot of time and patience. They need to be walked, and played with, and they take up more than their fair share of the bed at night. Dogs are wonderful. But they're also a very big commitment.

That being said, I am literally surrounded by canines. All of my siblings have dogs, and the same goes for my parents. So, I spend a lot of time dog-sitting for the people in my life. I feed their fur babies when they go out of town, I walk their pets when they work late, and I share my home with four-legged friends whenever the situation requires.

Currently, I'm watching my sister's dog. Having him here has been a huge change in my daily routine. I like to sleep late whenever I get the chance, but every morning he demands to be walked as soon as the clock says 6 am. At first, this caused a lot of frustration on my part. However, having him here has taught me many important lessons about Right View.

The three biggest ones are:

## SURRENDER TO THE FORM

When I walk into my Zen center, there are countless forms that I must follow. There are correct and incorrect ways to bow to Buddha, etiquette that must be followed when addressing the monks, and rituals that must be observed when getting up from the cushion.

These forms can be overwhelming. However, I've learned that if I surrender to them, and simply do what needs to be done in the moment, a feeling of contentment arises in my mind  Furthermore, I've learned that daily life is also full of forms.

There are forms that I must follow when I go to work regarding dress codes and client meetings. There are forms for gardening and bike maintenance. And there are countless forms that go with caring for a dog. Life is full of forms, and when I surrender to them in the same way that I surrender to the forms inside of my Zen center, life becomes much easier.

## COMPASSION COMES FROM HUMILITY

I care for dogs who treat the whole world as their toilet. And I deal with others who are more particular about where they do their business. In both cases, however, I'm responsible for the aftermath.

Thankfully, scooping up dog poop from the sidewalk and scrubbing pee out of a carpet both make for excellent Buddhist practice. I'm humbled each time I walk down the street with a leash in one hand, and a bag of manure in the other. And I learn a lesson in karma when a dog leaves "presents" on the carpet because I waited a too long before taking them out.

All of this has shown me how humility and compassion intersect. The dogs in my care are sentient beings, and I want to take good care of them. But I can't do that unless I humble myself and become their servant. That means I must grab the leash every time they want to go for a walk, and I must fill their food bowl every evening before I fill my own. If I do anything less, they'll suffer as a result.

## DESIRE IS A SOURCE OF SUFFERING

It's a little frustrating for me to write this part. After thousands of hours on the cushion, one would think that I'd understand this point in my bones. But I still need to be reminded of it every day. and dogs are excellent at doing that. As I stated earlier, my sister's dog absolutely must be walked at 6 am every day. He has a small meltdown if it doesn't happen.

This was a point of intense suffering for me the first week that he was here, but then I realized something. It's 100 percent normal and natural for him to want to pee in the morning. I do it, so why shouldn't he? Furthermore, it's not his fault that he lives in a house, and not in the wilderness like nature intended. So, what right do I have to be mad at the dog for something that's both completely natural and not his fault?

I don't have that right. And the suffering that I experienced had nothing to do with him. It was caused by my desire to lounge in bed. Instead of surrendering to the form and walking the dog, I was surrendering to my ego, and I suffered as a result. These days I simply go to bed a bit earlier in preparation for our morning stroll. That works much better than complaining.

**Lesson:** Buddha wags his tail and walks on four legs.

# Right Intention

# Turning the TV Off

Right Intention is the second tenet of the Noble Eightfold Path. It represents the strong resolve that practitioners develop to end suffering for themselves and others when they walk the Buddhist path. On the surface, this seems like a no-brainer. No one wants to suffer, and everyone hopes for a peaceful life. So, why is Right Intention necessary?

An easy way to think about it is to imagine a small child who stays up past his bedtime to watch TV. He must wake up early to go to school, and he knows it. He also knows that he'll be tired and cranky all day if he doesn't get enough sleep. But he's so caught up in his desire to watch TV that he doesn't care. Things like "waking up early" and "getting enough rest" are too abstract, too far off into the future to matter. But his TV show is right here in front of him. And it's real, and it's fantastic, and he can think of nothing else. So, he stays up late, and he suffers as a result.

When we live in the mind of desire, we're just like the child watching TV. We know that our actions will have consequences. And sometimes we know what those consequences will be. But we're so caught up in the short-term pleasure of what we're doing that we don't care about who we hurt, even if the person we hurt is ourselves.

That's why Right Intention, which could also be called Right Vow is so important. It's a promise we make to ourselves and others that we'll prioritize the end of suffering over our desires. It represents our strong determination to grow in our Buddhist practice. In the Bible, 1 Corinthians, chapter 13: 11 states:

*When I was a child, I spoke as a child, I understood as a child, I thought as a child; but when I became a man, I put away childish things.*[13]

For Buddhists, sensual desires (wealth, status, animosity, etc.) are the "childish things" that we must put away. Right View helps us to see what those things are, and Right Intention gives us the strength to let them go. This happens in the same way that a child learns to turn off the TV and go to bed at a decent hour once they become an adult.

In his wisdom, Buddha taught that there are three types of vows that can assist us in the practice of Right Intention. They are as follows:

1. **Vows of renunciation** - These help us create strong determination to let go of actions and mental habits that cause harm to ourselves and others.
2. **Vows of goodwill** - These help us create strong determination to act in ways that create happiness for ourselves and others.
3. **Vows of harmlessness** - These help us create strong determination to act in ways that remove suffering from our life and the lives of others.

These practices are important because they help us counter the three poisons of greed, anger, and ignorance that cause human suffering. Renunciation counters greed, goodwill counters anger, and harmlessness counters ignorance. So, the tenet of Right Intention helps to extinguish the poisons in our heart and moves us closer to nirvana.

From a traditional, Buddhist standpoint, our vows may take the form of renouncing drugs and alcohol in our daily life or creating goodwill through the use of daily Metta (loving-kindness) meditations. In a more conventional sense, we may commit to giving five compliments to other people each day (goodwill) or refusing to argue with people on social media (harmlessness).

As our commitment to the Dharma grows, our commitment to Right Intention also grows. Eventually, our vows of renunciation, goodwill, and harmlessness stop being about Buddhism, and they shift to simple, daily habits that we enjoy. When this happens, we stop turning the TV off at night for fear of being tired. Instead, we turn it off because we enjoy getting a full night's rest.

**Lesson:** When we let go of short-term pleasure, we gain long-term happiness

## Train Travel and Dining Cars

My maternal grandfather worked for the railroad. When I was a kid, he used to give me cool swag (hats, duffel bags, pins, etc.) that he got from work. And once I was old enough to read, I would watch with rapt attention every time my family stopped at a train crossing, reading aloud the names on each train car in the hopes that I'd see one from papa's company. Between that and the countless train sets that I received for Christmas each year, I developed a love for the railroad that has persisted into adulthood.

And let's be honest, there's a lot to love when it comes to trains. There's the connection to history one feels when they sit in a train station, waiting to begin their journey as people have done for centuries. There's the sheer romanticism of traveling the rails and seeing parts of the country we never knew existed. And one can't help but marvel at the engineering prowess required to send 100 tons of steel train careening down the tracks while passengers sit quietly in their seats.

However, it's the people that make train travel truly special for me. I can think of few places outside of a train car where one meets such a large swathe of humanity. There are potato farmers on their way to Chicago to visit relatives and Amish people on their way to Florida for a funeral. One might sit next to a retiree set on spending his kid's inheritance before he dies or a middle schooler who's researching train travel for extra credit. Hippies, professionals, mothers, and drifters - if one rides the rails long enough, they'll run into them all.

This is important to note when one considers the food situation. Unlike an airplane where attendants deliver food to the passengers' seat, train riders must venture to the dining car for their meal. It's a pleasant experience overall, but there's one important caveat. Diners don't get to choose their dining companions. The rider goes to the dining car, speaks with the host, and then they're assigned to a table where three other strangers will also be seated. So, if one wants to ride the train, they need to be good at making friends. Because whether they like their fellow diners, or not, they still have to share a meal with them.

Thus, an unspoken code of conduct exists inside the dining car: Don't do anything that will ruin the meal. After all, we'll probably see our fellow riders again. We'll sit next to them in the observation car. We'll pass them in the aisle on the way to the restroom. And we'll stand in line with them on the train platform, waiting for our luggage.

There's no escape from the people we share meals with, so riders develop a strong commitment to "make it work" with everyone they meet regardless of race, religion, or political affiliation.

This is a beautiful practice, and it blends perfectly with the Buddhist tenet of Right Intention. After all, everyone lives in a dining car of some sort, surrounded by people we can't escape. Maybe it's the family members we see during the holidays or the coworkers we see at work. Perhaps our dining car is the line at an amusement park or the apartment complex that we share with other tenants. And let's not forget that all of humanity lives together on a giant dining car called Earth.

Living with Right Intention gives us the tools we need to live in these situations and "make it work" with everyone we meet. It's an acknowledgment that we're all in this together, and that personal happiness is only possible if we work for the happiness of others. So, we commit to being on our best behavior in daily life in the same way that we use good table manners when sharing a meal with strangers.

And as we move through life practicing renunciation, goodwill, and harmlessness, a natural blowback occurs. Taking the feelings of other people into account causes us to have positive life experiences. This happens in the same way that not chewing with our mouth open allows for pleasant dinner conversation.

In this way, it doesn't matter if we're stuck in a dining car, or an office building, or a traffic jam with other people. Because regardless of who we meet, we're resolved to "make it work" for ourselves and others. Thus, life becomes a bit more pleasant, and everyone gets to enjoy their meal.

**Lesson:** Life is a dining car, make it work

# Sibling Rivalry

I have a very large family. My father is one of 16 children, and my mom is one of four. When they got married, they had five children together in addition to one daughter that my dad had in his first marriage. So, I have five brothers and sisters along with a seemingly endless number of aunts, uncles, and cousins. In fact, one of the best parts of family reunions is meeting new relatives for the first time and running into others I haven't seen in years.

Of course, like all big families, we have disagreements, and sometimes those fights can be heated, but they always seem to get settled over a homecooked meal and an aunt demanding that everyone "hug it out." However, there was one sad exception to this rule for a long time.

One of my younger sisters and I started arguing around the time I turned 15, and the fight lasted well into my late early 30s. Any number of things could set us off. I would use the wrong facial expression with her; she would use the wrong tone of voice with me; it would be Thursday. The reason didn't matter. It was just understood that if we were around each other for too long, fireworks would be the result.

Eventually, it got bad enough that I didn't want to attend family gatherings if I knew she'd be there. And when I did attend gatherings when she was present, our fighting would ruin the event for everyone else. Something had to change.

When I started practicing Buddhism, my study of the sutras made it clear that our fights weren't in keeping with the practice. We were causing suffering for the people around us and causing harm to each other. As I thought about it, I realized that I couldn't control my sister's behavior, but I could control my own. So, I made the vow that I wouldn't fight with her anymore.

If things got bad, I would remove myself from the situation (renunciation). Otherwise, I promised myself that any time I wanted to lash out, I'd either remain silent (harmlessness) or give a compliment instead (goodwill).

I enjoy making ritual part of my practice, so to do this in such a way that I couldn't go back on my promise in the heat of the moment, I made my vow part of my evening meditation. Each night when I finished sitting, and I recited the bodhisattva vows, I added a fifth vow to the ceremony that went as follows:

1. Living beings are numberless; I'll work to benefit them
2. Delusions are endless; I'll see through them
3. The teachings are infinite; I'll learn them
4. The Buddha way is difficult; I'll walk the path
5. I don't care what she says to me; I won't fight with my little sister

Of course, it's one thing to set a strong intention. But it's another thing to carry it out. One thing that shocked me about this practice was how much it revealed about me and the role I played in our constant bickering. I was surprised by the amount of anger that came up in me at what now seemed to be innocuous looks or phrases.

Looking back, I had a lot of mental hang-ups around how she was supposed to treat me as a big brother. "Who the hell does she think she is talking to me that way," was a common thought that popped into my head. But to keep my vow, I had to let that question and those feelings go. Whatever she said in the heat of the moment was exactly that - what she said. My only job was to respond with harmlessness and goodwill.

It was slow-going. There were a lot of hurt feelings that had built up between us over the years. At first, I think she thought it was a trick. Next, I think she was just confused. But as the weeks turned into months and eventually years of me either remaining silent, offering a compliment, or simply walking away from arguments, she opened up.

It was as if my taking a step back gave her the breathing room to also take a step back. And once there was a little distance between us, we could see each other more clearly. All the compliments I gave her reminded me that she had a ton of good qualities that I'd overlooked because of my anger. She's smart, attentive to detail, and masterful at organizing family gatherings.

Eventually, my sister started asking me if I wanted to hang out and calling me when she needed advice. We bonded over our love of food and Netflix original series, and now we're good friends.

There are two things that I learned from this experience. First, I learned that Right Intention is useless unless we back it up with *strong* intention, an unbreakable resolve to keep going no matter what. If I had given up after the first time or the 200<sup>th</sup> time that my sister lashed out at me, we'd still be where we were before, fighting constantly over nothing.

Second, I learned that when it comes to Right Intention, we must value our vows more than our ego. It's one thing to promise that we'll do the right thing. But living up to that promise is hard work. In fact, I have a sneaking suspicion that no one wants to hurt other people. No one wants to steal, lie, or fight with their family members. But they find a reason to justify those actions. And they suffer as a result

There were times when I felt angry, hurt, or even embarrassed because of the things that were said to me. And a million justifications popped into my head about why I should let it all out "just this once." But the Dharma was more important to me than winning an argument. I valued my practice more than my ego. So, I was able to keep my vow. More importantly, I got my sister back.

**Lesson:** Do the right thing, even when it's hard.

## Enlightened Earlobes

Iconography is an important part of Buddhist practice. There are many reasons for this, the first being that humans like symbols, religious and otherwise. Whether it's the wedding ring on the finger of a new bride or the American flag being displayed at the start of a sporting event, symbols take abstract ideas like faith, love, tradition, etc.

and turn them into something real. They allow us to pick up our ideals and hold them in our hands.

In addition to that, symbols are terrific teaching tools. It might take years to write, edit, and publish a text that explains complex religious maxims. However, the proper use and placement of religious icons can explain those same maxims with significantly less effort. Examples of this exist in Buddhism, which has the eight-spoke wheel (representing the Noble Eightfold Path) and the lotus flower (representing enlightenment). Another icon that's found in Buddhist centers are statues of the Buddha, depicting him in seated meditation.

These statues serve several purposes. First, they act as a physical representation of our inherent enlightenment. Second, they depict both the historical Buddha and the 2,600 years of Buddhist tradition that formed after his death. So, when we light incense, make offerings, or bow in front of an altar that possesses a Buddha statue, we are paying homage to our inherent enlightenment, Buddhism as a whole, and the historical Buddha simultaneously. How's that for efficiency?!

The physical attributes of each statue will vary. For example, one may show the Buddha holding a begging bowl while another may show him with his hands in the universal mudra. However, almost all of them depict him as having elongated earlobes. And there's an important reason for this.

Before the Buddha became a holy man, he was a Hindu prince who lived in the lap of luxury. As was common in those days, he probably wore a lot of expensive jewelry (e.g., gold rings, necklaces, earrings, etc.) while he lived in the palace. This would serve two purposes.

First, it would let everyone know at a glance that he came from a wealthy and powerful family. Second, the jewelry acted as a forced savings account. If he ever had to flee for his life with nothing but the clothes on his back. His jewelry would automatically go with him, ensuring that he had enough wealth to start over somewhere new.

For this reason, princes wore heavy, gold earrings that stretched their earlobes over time. However, a close inspection of a Buddha statue reveals that he isn't wearing earrings or jewelry of any kind. He removed all of it as part of his renunciation practice.[14] This was a big deal; the modern equivalent would be someone burning their social security card and giving away all of their money before going on a spiritual journey.

By removing his earrings, Buddha made it clear that he had no intention of returning to palace life. More than that, he was refusing to rely on material goods for safety and security. It was this insistence on living life without a safety net that helped him realize enlightenment. And the elongated earlobes that we find on Buddha statues are a reminder of his dedication.

**Lesson:** Don't be afraid to let go!

## Lessons from a Racist Buddha

People look at me strangely when I say racism doesn't bother me. They seem confused when I, a black man, shrug and continue about my business while they rant about the latest person caught wearing blackface, shouting the N-word, or accosting people of color for the simple crime of existing.

Of course, I know the response they're expecting. They want me to throw things, to yell, and maybe even cry a little. They want me to act out in ways that will give them some catharsis, that will reinforce their goodness in being outraged on my behalf. But I don't do that. I don't do that because of a quote from James Baldwin, which states:

> *To be a Negro in this country and to be relatively conscious is to be in a rage almost all the time.*[15]

Baldwin was a fiction writer and social critic who rose to prominence during the civil rights movement of the 1960s and '70s. His book of essays, *The Fire Next Time,* was one of my favorite reads in college. And the documentary *I Am Not Your Negro* by Raoul Peck gives terrific insight into the mind of this great American writer.

I agree with Baldwin's assessment. To be the least bit conscious of racism in America is to fall victim to a deep, unending rage. But we can't stop there. We can't let the conversation end with outrage. Rather, we must ask ourselves two questions. First, where does this rage come from? Second, what are we going to do about it?

In my experience, the rage that Baldwin speaks of comes from a feeling of despair that manifests when the people and institutions we love don't love us back. I've felt this despair many times in my life. I felt it when a girl I used to date told me I couldn't come to her birthday party because her "old-fashioned" grandma was going to be there, and she didn't like black people. I felt it again when a "woke" activist who I considered a friend started making jokes like "Open your eyes, Alex. It's dark, and we can't see you."

Of course, these aren't the only incidents of racism that I've witnessed/experienced in life. From the death of Heather Heyer at the hands of a white nationalist in Charlottesville, Virginia, to the slaying of Tamir Rice in Cleveland, Ohio, American history is littered with reasons for despair going back to our country's founding. And if one isn't careful, that despair grows into the constant, all-encompassing rage that James Baldwin described.

However, Buddhism is clear that anger (even when it's justified) is a poison. It tears us apart from the inside and does little to solve the problem at hand. In fact, the fifth-century Buddhist scholar Buddhagosa spoke of anger by saying:

> *By doing this, you are like a man who wants to hit another and picks up a burning ember or excrement in his hand and so first burns himself or makes himself stink.*

Visuddhimagga IX, 23.[16]

Frankly, I don't think covering myself in metaphorical excrement is a healthy response to racism. So, while the despair, pain, and inevitable anger that comes from racism is justified, I've learned to let it go over the years.

Instead, I use these incidents as a reminder that even though I love America for the food, clothing, and shelter that is has provided me over the years, there are certain things this country can't give me. If I want to be validated as a human being, one who isn't used as a Halloween costume, I'll have to look elsewhere for that.

So, that answers the question "Where does rage come from," but we still need a decision on what to do about it.

For me, Buddhism has been a saving grace in this regard. It's been the practice that has nourished me, sustained me, and protected my mental health in the face of one racist incident after another. It has done this by showing me that the true cause of racism is the illusion of a separate self, which comes from ignorance. So, as long as ignorance exists in the world, racism will also exist.

Oddly, I find comfort in this teaching. It keeps me from taking things so personally. Instead, I grimly accept the existence of racism in the same way that I accept icy roads in winter or a sore back during meditation. I don't like it, but I must learn to live with it.

In this way, the "racist Buddhas" that pop up every few weeks in the form of old college photos and chants of "Jews will not replace us," teach me equanimity, pushing me deeper into my practice. They remind me that lasting peace can't be found in the conventional world, so I must seek it out in the spiritual one.

It's there, on my cushion, that I find the shining jewel of Dharma, 2,600 years of Buddhist tradition that has sustained practitioners in the face of unfathomable suffering. It helped the Tibetans when they were driven from their country by Chinese occupiers. It protected Dogen when the river near his monastery was filled with dismembered body parts.

And it supports me in every moment that the world causes me to despair. Racism doesn't bother me because I have something that racism can never touch. I have the Dharma. And it will always hold me up, even when people let me down.

**Lesson:** When Samsara hurts, take refuge in the Dharma

# Right Speech

# Right Speech and MAGA Hats

The internet is ablaze with sound and fury. In fact, I had to shut off my phone last night because it wouldn't stop buzzing from all the Facebook and Twitter notifications that I was receiving. Apparently, some crazy stuff happened in Washington DC over the weekend.

The short version is that a group of students from Covington, Kentucky, were standing on the steps outside of the Lincoln Memorial. The kids had just finished attending the March for Life, and some of them were wearing MAGA hats. At some point, they got into a shouting match with Black Hebrew Israelites who were standing nearby, which led to the students engaging in a school chant.

Amid all this, a Native American elder who was in DC for the Indigenous People's March walked into the crowd, began beating his drum, and chanting a sacred song. The kids responded by continuing their chants. It should have ended there.

But a short video was released of the incident. Then several longer videos were released that provided more details as to the chain of events. As a result, the last few days have been a weird mix of people blaming the kids, apologizing for blaming the kids, venerating the Native American elder, saying that the elder is partially to blame and debating the historical accuracy of Black Hebrew Israelites.

I have a lot of strong opinions about this incident and the issues involved. I have opinions about the pro-life movement, MAGA hats, and indigenous rights. But I'm not going to share any of those opinions here. I'm not going to share them because nearly 72 hours after this altercation happened my phone is STILL buzzing with notifications from people who want to get the last word in.

In my experience, if one finds himself in a room filled with screaming people, it's best to be the one silent person. At the very least, it keeps a bad situation from becoming worse. So, I apologize if anyone is hoping that this essay will feed their rage-addiction, but I'm not throwing more fuel on the fire. Instead, I'm going to discuss the Buddhist teaching of Right Speech, and how it can help us in times like this.

On the surface, the teaching of Right Speech is simple. I've heard it explained as "Be polite, and don't start trouble." That's a good start, but the teaching goes much deeper than that. When Buddhists practice Right Speech, we strive to ensure that our words fall into one of two categories:

1. They actively remove suffering from the world (compassionate-action)
2. They actively add joy and contentment to the world (loving-kindness)[17]

Compassionate-action and loving-kindness are two of the four awakened mind states that Buddhism encourages us to develop. The other two are sympathetic joy and equanimity. The teaching of Right Speech states that as long as our words fall under either compassionate-action or loving-kindness, then they'll naturally lead the people around us and us to experience sympathetic joy and equanimity.

For example, I was at dinner with my family the other night when I found out my nephew had a good report card (five As and one B). He's very smart, and his report cards are always good, but I wanted him to know that I appreciate his hard work.

So, I waited until everyone gathered around, and then I made a point of telling him (loudly) how proud I was of him (loving-kindness). He responded by smiling ear to ear. His happiness made me and the rest of the family happy, and a teacher who happened to be sitting nearby came over to congratulate him as well (sympathetic-joy). Finally, at various points during the day when I felt bothered by what happened in Washington, DC, thinking about my smart, happy nephew calmed me down (equanimity).

There are two things that we can take from this example. First, the awakened mind states feed into each other, so developing one helps us to develop the others. Second, Right Speech isn't just about using kind words. It's about actively using our words to create healthy mind states in ourselves and others.

In other words, if we're feeling scared, angry, anxious, confused, etc. because of what happened in Washington DC, one Buddhist method for dealing with those emotions would be to speak words of compassion and loving-kindness to others. Speaking from experience, the more we engage in Right Speech, the better we feel.

So, coming back to my original point. I have a lot of opinions about what happened in DC. I have even more opinions on what I've read/ watched on social media. But the only thing I'm going to say is this:

May everyone be happy.

May everyone be healthy.

May everyone be safe.

I love you.

**Lesson:** If you don't have something nice to say, say something nice anyway.


## Breaking the Cycle of Wrong Speech

There was a two-year period of my life where I had no social media accounts. I forget what spurred the change, but one day I got fed up and just deleted all my accounts. There were some minor difficulties. I sometimes missed out on party invites because everything was coordinated on Facebook. And I missed out on all of the "dank" memes that took over the internet. But overall, I'd say that was one of the most peaceful periods of my life.

Granted, I spent eight months of that time in retreat, living, working and meditating on organic farms where I had no internet access. So, keeping my "no social media" vow was easy during that time. For the rest of it, I just learned to be comfortable with not knowing every detail of everyone's life. I trusted that if it were important, they'd find another way to tell me.

But that was several years ago, and like the cell phones that came before, social media has shifted from a fun toy to a near necessity for anyone living in the modern age. We find jobs through LinkedIn, we get our news through Twitter, and we rely on Facebook to help us keep track of birthdays (at least I do).

So, if we are going to live in the world as Buddhists, then we need to learn how to use social media skillfully, in a way that's in accordance with the Dharma.

This can be hard to do. It's easy to write-off the things we say online as "just" a tweet or an email. But we must remember that what we're talking about is speech. And what we post online can be just as helpful or hurtful to our fellow humans as the words we write in a book or say aloud. Sadly, much of the language that one finds on social media pages falls into the category of wrong speech, which the Buddha described as anything that falls into the following categories:

1. False speech
2. Divisive speech
3. Abusive speech
4. Speech that is idle chatter[18]

So, it's incumbent on us to ensure that any posts that we allow on our feeds do not fall into one of these four categories. Doing so frees us of our defilements and helps to prepare our minds for other practices like chanting and meditation. It's also an effective way to reduce the amount of suffering that exists in the world. But if we want to reap these positive benefits, we have to do two things:

1. Avoid making posts that fall into one of the four categories of wrong speech
2. Avoid sharing or retweeting posts that fall into one of the four categories of wrong speech

When we do this, we break the cycle of wrong speech, ensuring that other people aren't exposed to hurtful or divisive commentary. This allows us to practice compassionate-action by keeping a post that causes suffering from moving through the interwebs.

Of course, that doesn't mean that other people won't hit the "share" button as quickly as their fingers allow. But we can't be responsible for the actions of other people. We can only be responsible for our actions and the consequences that come from them. And if we're unsure whether we should share or retweet a post, we only need to ask ourselves two questions:

1. How did this post make me feel?
2. Do I want other people to feel this way?

If the answer to either question is a negative one, then we shouldn't share it with our friends and loved ones. Instead, we should simply scroll past it, and let the post's negativity disappear into the sea of internet anonymity.

**Lesson:** The cycle of wrong speech is broken one internet post at a time.


## A Buddhist Take on Valentine's Day

Yesterday was Valentine's Day, and as I watched people either celebrate the love in their life or mourn the lack of it, I found myself wondering, "What is the nature of love?" After all, everyone is talking about it, but no one seems to know what it is. But I think it's fair to say that Americans have some unhealthy concepts around the ideas of love and relationships.

For us, love is attachment-based, almost to the point of obsession. We want to be the center of someone's world to the point that they can't live without us. And we measure their love (or lack thereof) by the amount of stuff they give us on Christmas, birthdays, and Valentine's Day.

The result can be one of sadness and frustration if we don't have someone who makes us feel like the center of the universe. And even if we have that special someone, a lot of heartache can occur if they don't live up to the expectations set by the $20 billion Valentine's Day industry.

This is all quite problematic. In fact, it's led some of history's greatest philosophers to wonder if love even exists or is it just a chemical reaction in our brains that corporations exploit to sell merchandise. From the Buddhist perspective, love is most definitely real. However, it doesn't exist in the way that Americans imagine. Buddhist love is deeply impersonal, more than that, it's universal.

To understand this apparent contradiction, we must first define the Buddhist concept of love. Traditionally, it's broken into two parts. There's compassion, which is the active removal of suffering from our lives. And there's loving-kindness, which consists of the active addition of happiness to our lives. Thus, any person, animal, or object that removes suffering or adds joy to our existence is expressing a deep love and affection for us.

In this way, Buddhist love is impersonal because we don't have to do anything to receive it. It's not based on our looks or our bank accounts. And we literally can't make it go away because the universe is constantly expressing its love for us. We just have to train our eyes to see it.

This is the love of a tall tree that gives us shade on a hot summer day. It's the love of a light bulb that lets us read a favorite book long into the night and a comfy bed that keeps us warm when it's cold outside. And yes, Buddhist love is also the partner who cuddles in that bed with us. But whether we have a partner, or not, in Buddhism, we are always loved.

When we open our eyes and take note of the countless ways that the universe either removes suffering (compassion) or adds joy (loving-kindness) to our lives, we realize how special we must be if we're surrounded by so much goodwill. Our feeling of lack is replaced with a feeling of wholeness. And we learn how to express this universal love to others.

In every word, and every gesture we tell the world, "I love you." And in every moment of every day, the world says, "I love you," back.

**Lesson:** Every day is Valentine's Day if we're paying attention.

## Healing Words

In Mahayana Buddhism, a Bodhisattva is an awakened being who refuses to enter nirvana until all sentient beings can come with them. With immeasurable compassion, they choose to live in samsara, working endlessly to heal the suffering of our world. One example of a Bodhisattva would be Kannon, the Bodhisattva of compassion. She is often depicted riding a dragon, standing in a position of perfect calm as ocean waves crash around her, and a full moon shines in the sky. Kannon listens to the piteous cries of our world, and she radiates compassion in response.

But how does she radiate that compassion? More importantly, does her radiance make a difference? These are the questions that fill my head as I look upon her image. As I've pondered these things over the years, I've come to some conclusions. First, Kannon radiates compassion through her example. It's been my experience that when everyone else in the room is panicking, it's beneficial to remain calm. Sometimes bringing soothing energy to a situation is all that's needed to lower the tension between people. And one certainly feels a sense of calm when they see Kannon standing serenely amid a storm.

Second, I believe the bodhisattva of compassion uses Right Speech to ease the suffering of our world. After all, if she can hear the cries of the downfallen, it seems strange that she wouldn't respond. Thus, her radiance takes the form of healing words that make people feel seen, heard, and appreciated. This is something that we've all experienced in our personal lives. When someone says, "I'm sorry for your loss," after the death of a loved one, their words lessen our pain. And when we're sick, in bed with the flu, receiving a card that says, "Get well soon," brings a smile to our face.

These words are helpful because they remind us that we're not alone. They express empathy and confirm that there's someone out there who cares. In this way, Right Speech negates the suffering of the world. It makes life easier to bear. And that's why the example of the Kannon is so powerful because her practice is something that all of us can do.

Each of us can be a bodhisattva of compassion. We can radiate calm during difficult situations. And we can offer healing words in times of distress. In this way, each time we speak with empathy, Kannon speaks through us.

But that leaves us with my second question. Do these kind words make a difference? Well, to answer that we first need to understand the symbolism that exists in Kannon's image. The moon shining in the sky represents enlightenment. The crashing waves represent the suffering of the world. And the dragon, a very auspicious symbol, represents the wisdom of Buddha's teachings.

So, the moon shines on Kannon, and Kannon shines in the world. Standing amidst suffering, she brings light into the darkness, helping us walk the Buddhist path. But even in her presence, the waves don't disappear. If there's an ocean, there will be waves. And if there's samsara, there will be suffering.

Kannon knows this, but she shines her light anyway. And that's what makes her special. The bodhisattva of compassion sets her shoulder to the wheel, vowing that even if she can't do everything, she'll still do everything she can.

Likewise, when we offer healing words in daily life, we don't try to end the world's suffering in one fell swoop. Rather, our goal is to bring the light of Dharma into dark places and assist others in finding the path.

So, the practice works in that it eases the suffering of others and helps them on the path to enlightenment. But it comes with one important caveat. If we want our words to heal people, we must walk into the waves, and speak.

**Lesson:** Be a light in the darkness. Speak healing words.

## Right Listening and Jazz Improvisation

One aspect of Right Speech that often gets ignored is the importance of Right Listening. After all, it's impossible to have healthy, healing conversations with people if we don't focus in on what's being said.

To do this, we first need to understand the difference between hearing and listening. Hearing only requires that we have functioning ears that pick-up sound waves in our environment. Listening, however, requires us to pay attention and comprehend what those sounds are saying.

Jazz musicians are great listeners. The performers "talk" to each other throughout their sets with players using changes in rhythm or certain sets of notes to signal what's coming next. For example, the lead player might play a pre-selected riff to signal the end of a song. And a drummer might change up his syncopation to let a solo artist know that it's time to perform.

Occasionally, multiple band members will play solos at the same time. When this happens, the expected result would be a lot of jumbled noise, but when experienced jazz players improvise, the result is magical. This happens because they don't just play at each other; they play with each other. They take the time to listen.

The trombonist listens to the drummer to decide if he should speed up or slow down his tempo. The saxophonist watches the guitar player to decide if he should play a harmony or a melody. And everyone pays attention to the leader so that they'll know when it's time to wrap up their solos and return to a jazz standard. This continuous conversation between the musicians plants the seeds for a great performance. And their intense focus on each other leads to a standing ovation.

Sadly, most of us don't listen very well. Sure, we're able to hear well. We know the other person is talking. And we politely wait for our turn to speak. But we have a hard time listening in the same way that musicians listen to their bandmates. There are many reasons for this. Some are cultural, and some are psychological. But the main reason is that each of us harbors a certain amount of self-centeredness.

In our weaker moments, we want the discussion to be all about us. So, we sit in our corner of the world and talk until someone rudely interrupts. Then we wait impatiently until we see our chance (e.g., the other person stopping to take a breath) and then we start speaking again. The result is two people making a lot of sounds without communicating. This makes Right Speech impossible.

Another way to think about it is to picture ourselves sitting in a dark room with a flashlight. If we see our own words and thoughts as being the most important, we'll keep the light pointed at our face. This ensures that we're the center of attention, but it stops us from seeing other people in the room. If we want to practice Right Speech, we must take the light off of ourselves and point it at someone else.

Jazz players do this all the time. They don't just play in the hopes of hearing their own music. Yes, that's part of it. But they also play to support each other. The pianist doesn't compete with the saxophone. Instead, he provides an accompaniment so that both musicians can play well together. But for this to happen, both musicians have to give up their self-centeredness. When they do this, they're able to pay attention to their bandmates and respond accordingly.

Thankfully, there are many techniques for becoming an effective listener. For example, in his book *Why Don't We Listen Better*, Dr. James Petersen encourages readers to start by acknowledging what the other person has just said, and then repeating it back to them.[19] This shows the other person that we're paying attention along with letting them clarify anything that we misheard. More than that, it forces us to take the flashlight off ourselves. After all, we can't accurately repeat back what was said if we're playing on our cell phones.

When we engage in this practice of Right Listening, we start a relationship with the people around us. Like musicians in a band, we play off of them, constantly gauging whether the moment requires us to speak or remain silent. This creates fertile ground for a conversation to develop and creates the necessary conditions for Right Speech.

**Lesson:** Always listen before you speak

# Right Action

# Gardening and the Bodhisattva Vows

One of my earliest experiences with growing food came when I practiced at a Zen center that had a garden. In Zen, manual labor is considered an important part of spiritual development, so I spent every Saturday cutting grass, pulling weeds, and shoveling horse manure into vegetable beds. "Shovel shit and become a Buddha!" was the running joke between me the other students. It was difficult at times, but there was a brutal honesty in the work that I found appealing.

If I cared for the plants properly, they would grow and provide food for people. If I didn't, they would die, and I'd have to start over from scratch. There was no complexity or intrigue involved in the process. What I put into the vegetable beds was exactly what I took out. It was karma in its purest form.

These days, I have a garden in my backyard. And I'm happy to report that the plants are still teaching me the Dharma. Lately, they've been teaching me about the bodhisattva vows which go as follows:

-Living beings are numberless, I'll work to benefit them
-Delusions are endless; I'll see through them
-The teachings are infinite, I'll learn them
-The Buddha way is difficult; I'll walk the path

The first thing any sane person notices about these vows is that they're impossible. How are you supposed to save all sentient beings if there is an infinite number of them? Thankfully, my plants have shown me the way.

144

The most important and time-consuming part of gardening is pulling weeds. If you don't do it regularly, the weeds will crowd out anything you are trying to plant, so consistency is key. However, there have been many times where I spent hours crawling through the dirt, pulling out invasive plants only to get up and wonder if I accomplished anything.

But I keep doing it because the small amount of time between when I pull the weeds and when they return gives my garden time to grow. Eventually, the vegetables become strong enough that they start crowding out the weeds!

Similarly, when we walk the bodhisattva path, we do so knowing that it's impossible. But we keep trying because each time we pull the "weeds" of greed, anger, and delusion from the world it provides space for "vegetables" like empathy and compassion to grow. Eventually, compassion grows large enough that it crowds out the darker parts of human nature, but only if we're willing to keep pulling weeds.

There is a brutal honesty in this work that I find appealing. The world is our garden, and what we put into it is exactly what we get out. Every act of kindness, no matter how small, provides space for good things to happen. And each time we help another person, we create an opportunity for their compassion to grow. It's hard work, and the struggle is never-ending. But a good harvest is guaranteed if we never give up.

**Lesson:** Right Action creates space for vegetables to grow

# Lessons from Bonsai Trees

The Japanese art of Bonsai originated from the Chinese practice of Penjing. Starting in the sixth century, Buddhist monks journeyed to China, and during the cultural exchange that took place, they learned about container plantings.

Over time, Japanese Buddhist aesthetics blended with the use of container plants in daily life to create Bonsai, which focuses on creating an idealized, miniature tree in an indoor setting. This is done using cultivation techniques like pruning, leaf trimming, defoliation, etc. I always admired bonsai trees from afar, but I never thought that I'd grow one myself.

That changed, however, when I realized that Enso, my cat, was hell-bent on ripping Sifu, my money tree, into tiny pieces. I thought I solved the problem by taking my tree to work and placing him on my desk, but that presented another issue. Money trees can grow up to 10 feet tall if they're cared for properly. And there's no way HR was going to approve a 10-foot-tall tree towering over my workstation. So, if Sifu was going to survive, he needed to remain small. Enter Bonsai.

I use poles and cords to shape the tree branches, scissors to trim the leaves, and my inner wisdom to decide what's needed in each moment. If too many leaves are cut away, Sifu will look sickly. If his branches are pulled in the wrong direction, he'll look unnatural.

The problem is complicated by the fact that technically Sifu isn't one tree. Rather, he's five trees that were planted together in one pot. This is common practice with money trees as the number five is considered lucky in Chinese culture.

Eventually, the various trees will merge into a single trunk, but until that happens, they'll compete for sunlight. If left to their own devices, they'd eventually crowd each other out, and most of them would die. So, pruning must be done regularly, and firm direction must be given. That's what Bonsai requires, that's what life demands. For Sifu to live, he must give up his attachments time and time again.

Human life works in the same way. We do what we want when we want, how we want under the pretense that we can enjoy freedom without enduring consequences. This is folly. Like a Bonsai tree, we suffer if we grow in every direction, chase after every delight. Instead, we must work to grow only in the right directions. And prune ourselves of every attachment that causes harm.

This is the purpose of Buddhist ethical training. The precepts are scissors that cut harmful actions from our lives. The Eightfold Path in wire and rope that straightens our branches, helping us move toward the light.

Like a skilled Bonsai master, Buddhism will strip us of everything that hinders our spiritual growth. But it can only do that if we're willing to let go. We must be willing to lose some leaves, trim some branches, and experience a bit of pain to reach our full potential.

So, this practice is not for the faint of heart. It takes strength to practice non-attachment. It takes courage to prune our spiritual selves. But if we can find it within us to obey the precepts, and walk the Eightfold Path, we'll be rewarded with a deep and abiding peace.

**Lesson:** Let go of desire and watch your practice grow!

# One Small Act

Most of us are familiar with the story of how Buddha realized enlightenment. Upon seeing that birth, aging, sickness, and death are all inescapable forms of suffering, he left his palace in the middle of the night, intent on finding the path to lasting peace. His journey lasted six years, and at the end of that time, he sat under the Bodhi tree and realized enlightenment. Afterward, he spent the next 45 years of his life teaching and practicing the Dharma until his death.

It's a beautiful story full of inspiration and heartache, and I haven't done it justice with the few sentences listed above. However, I want to make sure there's time to discuss part of the story that is often overlooked. That's the part about a peasant girl named Sujata.

Sujata was a milkmaid who lived in the town of Bakraur, located a few miles from Bodh Gaya where the Buddha happened to be staying. We aren't told much about her in the sutras other than that she wanted desperately to give birth to a child and had been praying fervently to a local tree spirit that she might be granted one. Eventually, her prayers were answered, and Sujata had a baby.[20]

Around this same time, Buddha was involved in a rigorous ascetic practice that required him to eat as little as possible. In fact, he was only eating one grain of rice a day, and he was so thin that he could poke his stomach and feel his spine through the skin. Needless to say, this was an unhealthy practice, and he was dying as a result.

At one point during his travels, he passed out from hunger and fell face first in a river. I imagine many people must have walked by him as he lay there. They were busy. They had important things to do. In the end, he just wasn't their problem.

But Sujata didn't walk by him. She saw someone in need, and she chose to act. Upon seeing his emaciated state, she mistook him for the tree spirit that had granted her a child, and she responded by giving him a meal of rice milk. The meal restored the Buddha's strength, and he lived. Of course, a single meal wouldn't be enough to restore a starved man to health. So, I imagine that Sujata returned the next day, and the day after that, feeding the man with the bony, tree-like limbs.

Perhaps she told him about her child, the one that brought her so much joy that she was compelled to help a stranger on the side of the road. Perhaps he told her about his journey and how he hoped to end suffering for all sentient beings. I like to think that these two people became good friends in the short time they spent together. But it's impossible to know for sure.

But we do know one thing for certain. Sujata saved Buddha's life. Due to her kindness, he didn't die face down in a river. Instead, he gave birth to a religion that currently has 535 million adherents worldwide.[21]

Sujata's story is important because it displays the power of Right Action. After all, she had no idea who the Buddha was when she saw him lying in the river. And there's no way she could have foreseen the impact this single man would have on the world. But she saw someone who was hungry. And she fed him. It was such a simple act, and yet 2,600 years later we're all benefitting from what she did.

As Buddhists, we must take this lesson and let it bleed into our daily life. Because when we think of Right Action, we often think about something grandiose. We want to start an orphanage, or plant a forest, or feed 1,000 starving people. But Sujata's story shows us that we don't need to "go big" to have an impact in the world.

We don't need to plant an entire forest. One tree will do just fine. And if we have the resources to feed 1,000 people, that's great. But feeding a single person is just as good because the echoes of our actions will sound through history long after we're dead.

The practice of Right Action is a practice of faith, a faith that says what we do matters. We matter. And whether we're refilling the coffee pot at work or speaking in front of a crowd of thousands, we have the power to change the world one small act at a time.

**Lesson:** One small act can change the world.

## Run Like a Buddhist

Most people know how to run. If they are in a hurry or something is chasing them, they know how to move their legs quickly. However, most people don't know how to run well. They either lack the endurance to run for a long period or the way they move their arms while running involves a lot of wasted motion. So, while one would be correct in saying that people with two working legs are inherently able to run. They'd also be correct in saying that people need to learn how to run correctly.

I know this from first-hand experience. My father was a track star in high school, and he competed at the state level well into his late 40s. One of the ways he spent time with my siblings and me was to take us running on a path near our house every Saturday. Rain or shine we'd run on the path for one mile, then we'd walk back, and he'd coach us on our technique.

As a result, phrases like "relax your shoulders" and "lift the knees and pump the arms" are permanently etched into my brain. Sometimes, my dad took it a step farther, and we'd drive to the local high school track where he'd videotape us running, going over the footage with us when we got home.

All of us children were physically healthy and inherently capable of running. But we needed a coach, my father, to help us run well. A similar relationship exists between Right Action and our inherent enlightenment. Each of us is an enlightened being in the same way that each of us is capable of running. But being enlightened and acting in an enlightened matter are two very different things. That's where the teaching of Right Action comes into play. It acts as a coach, showing us how to do enlightenment well.

When we vow to abstain from killing, lying, stealing, sexual misconduct, and the abuse of intoxicants, that doesn't make us better Buddhists. And it doesn't make us more worthy than people who don't take those vows. However, it creates conditions where our enlightenment can shine through us and create positive change in the world.

It's like sitting in a house at night. All of the lamps might be on, but people outside can't see the light if the curtains are closed. Right Action is the method we use to open the curtains and allow our inner light to go forth into the darkness.

More than that, it helps us to be proper image-bearers for the Dharma. In much the same way that we might watch champion marathoners to learn how to run, others can watch us to learn Buddhism. In this way, Right Action allows us to tap into our own divinity while simultaneously teaching others to do the same. In the end, it's not enough for us to talk like a Buddhist. We must live like one as well.

**Lesson:** Enlightenment is the practice of enlightened action

## Buddhist Liturgy

The dictionary defines liturgy as a collection of formularies for public worship.[22] Of course, one could be excused for not knowing what the word "formularies" means. I doubt that word is used very often outside of dictionaries. However, it translates simply to a collection or system of formulas[23].

So, when we discuss Buddhist liturgy, we're discussing formulaic actions that are done publicly in the hopes of creating a cohesive worship service. More than that, these actions create continuity within a tradition and build relationships among the participants.

Buddhist liturgy varies widely between traditions; however, they all involve the same basic tenets. Generally, it's only the amount that differs. For example, Soto Zen Buddhism places a heavy emphasis on Shikantaza or "just sitting" meditation. In contrast, Nichiren Buddhism is focused almost exclusively on the chanting of Daimoku (Namu Myōhō Renge Kyō). However, if one visits a Buddhist center, the liturgy will probably include the following: chanting, meditation, Dharma talks, and devotional practices like puja and prostrations. These rituals serve many purposes.

First, they unify the sangha. In the same way that a wedding creates a union between the families involved, a successful liturgy creates a familial bond between the members of a sangha. That's why students who take precepts together often refer to each other as "Dharma siblings". Of course, this results in Dharma aunts, cousins, and grandparents coming into the fold until an entire family tree develops with the newly inducted students resting on one of the branches.

Each time we perform the ritual with others, we strengthen the bonds within our Dharma family. The liturgy serves as a shared experience that each of us can draw from, uniting us in the face of race, class, and gender differences. This is something that I've experienced personally as I've traveled the country; visiting with fellow Buddhist teachers. A sense of calm comes over me when I notice similarities between their practice and my own. Whether we're lining our shoes up neatly by the door or chanting the Heart Sutra during practice, engaging in ritual with others makes me feel right at home.

Second, Buddhist liturgy allows us to practice Right Action in a safe, controlled environment. It hinges on the idea that if we act generously, then we'll naturally become more generous. And if we act peacefully, then we'll naturally become more peaceful. This may sound strange on the surface, playacting at emotions that we don't possess. But the connection between our actions and our emotional states is well documented in both science and literature. In fact, the American writer Kurt Vonnegut famously said, "Be careful what you pretend to be because you are what you pretend to be."[24]

Buddhist ritual allows us to pretend that we're kind, generous, loving people even when we don't feel that way. Over time, we learn to become the thing that we're imitating. For example, we learn generosity by performing puja, which involves giving food and incense offerings to the Buddha. Each time we place a cracker, an orange, or a lit candle on the altar, we give up a small part of ourselves. We do this once, twice, 10,000 times in the setting of a Buddhist temple until giving becomes as natural to us as breathing. Eventually, this newfound generosity spills out into our daily lives.

This is something that I've benefitted from personally. I'm not sure why, but generosity has never come easily to me. Before the Dharma found me, my thought process was that I wouldn't ask others for anything, they won't ask me for anything, and all of us will be happy as a result. But this is wrong thinking, rooted in the idea that there is a "me" and "them" who compete with one another. In contrast, Buddhism demands that we focus on the "us," and work to both give and receive from others with a happy heart.

Each time I stand in front of the altar, giving an offering of food or incense, my heart softens a little bit. This practice reminds me that I can give something away without the world falling apart. After doing this for several years, I've become more comfortable with giving my time, energy, and resources to people in need.

Another important part of Buddhist liturgy that helps us practice Right Action is seated meditation. This is the practice that Buddha used to realize enlightenment under the Bodhi tree, and it helps us to develop a mind of equanimity. In our modern world, we rarely have time to sit with our emotions and feel them. Instead, we're encouraged to constantly react to them either by distracting ourselves or feeding into them (e.g., we're angry, so we post a mean-spirited message on social media).

Through meditation, we act out equanimity, remaining perfectly still in the face of our emotions. Over time, space develops between them and us, and we stop being so responsive to them. Of course, this doesn't mean that we lose our capacity to feel. Buddhists experience pain, sadness, anger, etc. just like everyone else. But our training helps us to be less enthralled by our feelings. Our anger doesn't burn as hot. Our grief isn't quite so painful. And we heal faster, returning to a state of equanimity more quickly than we did before. Seated meditation is a key component in this.

Finally, liturgy provides a place of stillness as we move through life's daily storms. We can take comfort in the fact that these practices are enduring, having lasted for thousands of years. More than that, they give us something solid to hold onto as the world shifts around us. Our boss may be hard to work with, but our meditation cushion is always waiting when we get home. Our friends may turn on us, but Buddhists around the world are chanting and offering prayers on our behalf. In this way, Buddhist liturgy offers us security in an insecure world.

However, one doesn't have to be in a temple to engage in liturgical practice. For those who are interested, I've listed an interfaith Buddhist liturgy below that is simple, and easy to use. It includes influences from the Theravadin, Pure Land, and Zen Buddhist traditions, and it can be done anywhere, at any time.

**Recite Refuge Vows (1x):**

Budhham saranam gachhami,

Dhammam saranam gachhami

Sangham saranam gachhami

**Chant Nembutsu (9x):**

Namu Amida Butsu

**Seated Meditation (time varies from 1-108 minutes):**

1. Sit on the cushion
2. Close our eyes
3. Breathe
4. When our mind wanders, we gently bring our focus back to the breath

**Recitation of Bodhisattva Vows (1x):**

Living beings are numberless; I'll work to benefit them

Delusions are endless, I'll see through them

The teachings are infinite, I'll learn

The Buddha way is difficult; I'll walk the path

**Recitation of Refuge Vows (1x):**

Budhham saranam gachhami,

Dhammam saranam gachhami

Sangham saranam gachhami

For reference, these are the forms I use when practicing at my home altar. And depending on the amount of time one spends in meditation; the entire formulary can be completed in under 10 minutes. I've found that it has strengthened my practice and given me a sense of connection with my Dharma siblings all over the world.

**Lesson:** Don't just talk about Buddhism. Act it out through Buddhist liturgy

# Right Livelihood

# Everyone Has to Earn a Living

If Buddha was anything at all, he was a pragmatist. In fact, one of the key things that initially drew me to the Buddhist path was the logical step-by-step layout of the teachings. I've always been a process-oriented person, so I think the formal structures provided me with a sense of comfort early in my practice. And it was nice having a spiritual path that accounted for the practical needs of daily living.

For example, the Buddha understood that not everyone could walk the path of a monastic. For many of us, jobs, family duties, or simple lack of interest keep us from taking up the robes and bowl of a traditional Buddhist monk or nun. To account for this, Buddha designed a symbiotic system that allowed lay people and monastics to live with and support one another.

He did this by dividing the Buddhist sangha into four assemblies that consisted of monks, nuns, laymen, and laywomen. The monks and nuns were tasked with supporting the lay community's spiritual needs in the way of providing blessings, Dharma lessons, and setting a good example for them to follow. In return, the lay community was expected to provide the monks and nuns with material support in the way of robes, food offerings, and occasionally providing a place to live during the rainy season.

To ensure that they could devote 100 percent of their time to practicing Dharma, the monks and nuns did not hold jobs or practice agriculture. In addition to ensuring that they were able to focus on the practice, this also forced them to be 100 percent dependent on the lay community. So, there was lots of incentive to be a good representative of the Dharma. After all, if a monk was misbehaving, the community could respond by refusing to feed him!

Of course, this necessitated that the lay practitioners had jobs that not only provided for them and their families but also allowed them to have enough left over to give something to any monastics who came around for alms. Thus, the teaching of Right Livelihood was born.

Buddha understood that lay people needed the ability to earn a living and practice Buddhism at the same time. So, he created guidelines on how they could do both. When speaking of Right Livelihood he stated Buddhists should avoid the following professions:

1.  Weapons-dealing
2.  Slavery
3.  Animal Butchery
4.  Selling intoxicants
5.  Selling poisons[25]

It should be noted that in his wisdom, Buddha left a lot of room in terms of how people can support themselves. Instead of attempting to force lay people to earn money in very specific ways, he pointed out industries that were harmful to human welfare and instructed his followers to abstain from them. In this way, each person has a great deal of latitude in deciding how they wish to support themselves.

The relationship between Buddhist clergy and lay people has shifted quite a bit since this teaching was first given. Increasingly, Buddhist teachers are supporting themselves with full-time jobs in addition to teaching the Dharma. This is especially true in Western Buddhist circles, where there is no societal expectation that people will provide material support to the clergy.

This isn't a bad thing in and of itself. Buddhism is very malleable, shifting and molding itself to the needs of the individual. However, it does present certain challenges

For example, the demands of full-time employment make it difficult for Buddhists teachers to devote themselves 100 percent to practice in the same way that their forbearers did. After all, it's hard to do a three-month meditation retreat when one only has ten days of paid vacation each year.

As a result, one could argue that teaching Right Livelihood is even more important now than it was 2,600 years ago. Practitioners spend most of each day traveling to, preparing for, or engaging with their jobs each day. So, it's incumbent on them to find ways to integrate their jobs with their practice. This can be done in a variety of ways.

Of course, the first step is to act compassionately by abstaining from the five forbidden businesses listed above. After that, we can engage in traditional Buddhist practice in a variety of ways at work. We can chant when we get in our cars to leave at the end of the day. We can use Right Speech when conversing with our co-workers. We can read Dharma books during our lunch break. The possibilities are endless!

The key point is that we must be both creative and intentional to practice Right Livelihood because we don't need to be monastics to practice Buddhism correctly. We just need to strive in each moment to end suffering for ourselves and others, and how we earn a living in an important part of that goal.

**Lesson:** We can practice Buddhism and earn a living at the same time

## Save the Heater, Save the World

As a building apprentice, I had the opportunity to work on a wide variety of tasks. Sometimes I spent the entire day digging trenches for water pipes; other days, I poured concrete and installed wood fire stoves. Essentially, I was expected to be a jack-of-all-trades. Thankfully, Fred and Jack were both very skilled at this type of work, so they made up for the gaps in my knowledge.

One project involved working on a waste oil furnace in the community center. A waste oil furnace is a furnace that's designed to run used motor oil, and I had never seen one before my arrival at the farm. So, I was a bit worried when Jack showed it to Ed and me with instructions that said, "This is broken. It's going to be cold soon. Fix it." Based on this and other conversations, I think Jack may have been a Zen master in a previous life.

The furnace was a giant metal contraption that consisted of a large, 100-gallon reservoir that was bolted into the floor. It was rectangular in shape, and a large column rose four feet into the air from each corner of the reservoir, providing support for a much smaller metal housing unit at the top, which held the actual heater and the electronic parts. A metal chimney ran up to the ceiling, and a maze of pipes and plastic tubes ran between the reservoir and the housing unit.

After staring at the furnace in confusion for about ten minutes, Fred and I decided that neither of us had any idea what we were doing. So, I decided to fall back on my Labrador-like enthusiasm and hope for the best.

After poking around the community center for a while, we managed to find the manual, and praise Buddha, it included a checklist for troubleshooting the furnace if there were issues. First, we checked the reservoir and quickly determined that the furnace was low on oil. I called around to several auto shops in the area, and I found one that was willing to give us all the waste oil they had if we were willing to pick it up and had a way pump it into our barrels.

We dug around some more in the community center until we found a hand-powered drum pump that would (kind of) do the job along with a piece of plastic tubing and a metal clamp to hold the tube onto the pump's nozzle. Robert and I loaded three empty drum barrels into the back of his truck and headed over to the auto shop. We placed the pump in the shop's waste oil reservoir, inserted the plastic tube into one of the drum barrels, and began the arduous task of hand-pumping 55 gallons of oil into the drum

The connection between the tube and the pump leaked like crazy, so we got oil all over our hand and clothes, and we had to stop occasionally to retighten the clamp. But we managed to get the drums filled, and we headed back to the farm. Of course, that still left Fred and me with the fun task of hand-pumping the oil out of the drums and into the waste oil furnace.

But at this point, we were resigned to our fate. We put down newspaper to protect the community center floor from leaks and took turns pumping oil. I want to inject some mind-blowing tidbit at this point in the story about how my mind opened each time my hand cramped from the work, or we had to stop to clean up an especially bad leak. But I'd be lying. The truth is that this part of the process was mind-numbingly boring. But it needed to be done. So, I put my head down and practiced acceptance toward my boredom and grease-covered hands.

Acceptance is a big part of Right Livelihood. Society has us convinced that every moment of every day should be fun, sexy, and exhilarating. But when we add it all up, things usually don't work out that way. Most of life is the hard stuff, the boring, unsexy things that must get done. Life is sweeping floors, taking out the garbage, and washing the dishes.

Right Livelihood is waking up each day, going to work, and punching the clock because it needs to be done. It's practicing acceptance in the face of traffic jams, unruly co-workers, and paychecks that are never quite big enough. Of course, we work to improve our situation if we can. But sometimes that isn't possible. In those cases, we can hate it, or we can accept it, but we must do our job either way.

Once the reservoir was full, we attempted to crank on the furnace. It started running, but it didn't emit any heat. Disappointed, we returned to the user's manual, which directed us to a small window in the housing unit on top of the furnace.

According to the manual, if everything was working properly, fuel would be pulled from the reservoir where it would travel through pipes into the housing unit. From there, it would go through an atomizer, which would eject the fuel into a small chamber as a mist. Then the mist would be set on fire via a pilot light, generating heat that would be pushed out into the room via a fan. The window provided a way for us to safely look into the chamber and determine if the requisite mist and fire were being generated. They weren't.

So, we proceeded to dismantle the housing unit and clean every moving part with soap and water. From what we could tell this hadn't been done in quite some time as there was a lot of gunk and residue on the metalwork. As a result, the fuel wasn't flowing properly into the chamber, and no heat was being generated. The manual recommended a monthly cleaning schedule to keep this from happening, and after spending the better part of a day cleaning parts, Fred and I decided that we would follow this regiment to the letter.

Similarly, spiritual cleanliness is an important part of practicing Right Livelihood. Inevitably, as we go about our work, there will be grease and residue that accumulates in our mind. Perhaps we're mad at a coworker who threw us under the bus in a meeting. Or we may be under a lot of pressure to finish a project on time. This spiritual crud can gum up the metal works of our minds, keeping our natural goodness from flowing into the world. To stop this from happening, we must maintain a regiment that cleanses our minds of defilements, keeping everything in working order.

Thankfully, Buddhism provides many techniques for doing this. We can chant, read sutras, or practice meditation. To a certain extent, it doesn't matter what method we choose if we are consistent in its application.

After everything was cleaned and put back together, we attempted to turn on the heater again. Our hearts rose as a flame appeared in the housing unit's window, and they dropped just as quickly when the flame suddenly vanished. What happened?

Some more troubleshooting helped us determine that there was a small lever that determined how quickly fuel flowed through the atomizer. If the flow was too high or too low, the fire wouldn't burn consistently. So, we used trial and error with one of us looking through the window, and the other slowly adjusting the flow rate via the lever. It took some doing, but we eventually found the correct position for the level, which allowed the correct amount of fuel to flow into the atomizer. On what seemed like our 10,000$^{th}$ try, we turned on the heater, the flame didn't go out, and the community center filled with warmth.

We can draw two lessons from this. First, we must calibrate ourselves to put the appropriate amount of energy into our work. If the flow is too high, and we become a workaholic, then our flame will go out, just like the heater's flame went out when too much fuel flowed through the atomizer. Worse, we may neglect other, equally important parts of our lives like family, friends, and physical health.

On the other hand, if we put too little energy into our work, we won't be able to generate any flame. The quality of our work may be poor, resulting in unnecessary suffering for ourselves and others. Worse, we'll deny ourselves the satisfaction of completing a task with competence and skill.

So, we must always work to ensure that we don't fall into one of these two extremes. As long as we don't practice one of the forbidden professions (e.g., slavery, weapon sales, animal butchery, selling intoxicants, or selling poisons), then Right Livelihood demands that we work hard at our jobs, but not to the point that we sacrifice our physical health or family relationships.

The second lesson is that we shouldn't underestimate the amount of good we do each day simply by going to work. Between finding the oil, pumping it by hand, and then troubleshooting problems, it took Fred and me about two weeks to get the furnace up and running. It wasn't a fun or glamorous job. No monuments will be built for our efforts, and few people are even aware of what we did.

But our friends got to come inside every day during the winter and get warm because of our efforts. They ate, relaxed, and did aerial yoga once a week in a climate-controlled community center thanks to our hard work. And each time that heater kicked on, a little bit of suffering was removed from the world.

Similarly, most people don't have cool, sexy jobs in conventional society. And it can be easy to discount the amount of good we do in the world each day simply by going to work. But it's safe to say that if someone is willing to pay us for a task, then we must be making life better for someone. Otherwise, why would they pay us?

Whether it's the waitress who brings steaming hot food to a table of hungry people or the janitor who keeps an office clean and free of germs, each of us has the power to deliver joy and happiness to the people around us through the work we do. We may not receive monuments or high praise for our efforts, but we can take pride in the fact that our Right Livelihood is making the world a better place.

**Lesson**: Our jobs don't need to be glamorous to make a difference.

## Sacred Work

I had the good fortune of being a guest on the "Around Grandfather Fire" podcast with Jim Two Snakes and Sarenth Odinsson. We discussed several topics, including karma, ritual, and the integration of spirituality with daily life. It was the last point that got the conversation going. Because unless we choose to walk the monastic path, each of us must come to terms with the fact that our practice must include facets of mundane, ordinary life.

But that this isn't a new problem. When the first Buddhist missionaries came to China from India, they found a very different culture than what they were used to. There was no societal expectation that lay people would provide food and clothing to wandering holy men like there was in India. In fact, the Confucian government that was in place at the time persecuted Buddhist monks; seeing them as a threat to social order.[26] As a result, some of them returned to India, believing that "proper" Buddhism couldn't be practiced in this new land.

But some of those early missionaries stayed. And they began the difficult work of reshaping the teachings so that they could continue with their practice. They built temples, added more clothing to the traditional Buddhist robes for warmth, and they began practicing agriculture. This is also why Buddhist monks in China are vegetarian. Raising animals for food would require them to butcher those animals, which would violate both Right Livelihood and the first precept.

However, this change, which was initially made as a way for Buddhists to integrate their practice with the demands of daily life, has been romanticized over the years. It's not uncommon for people to look at monks laboring in the fields and think that this practice is "higher" or more suited to spirituality than the way they earn a living. In truth, it was a similar line of thinking that caused me to quit my job and begin working on organic farms.

I've since changed my thinking in this regard. And when I was explaining my reasoning for that to Jim, he made the following point:

> We've all had those same sorts of images that you see in media with the monk on the farm and that sort of thing. And I think people forget because it's easy to do in our modern context, but why were they working those fields? Because that was their job. That's how they fed themselves and their families, and their village. So, they developed those spiritual practices on their job, so to speak. And there's no reason why that same thing can't be applied to accounting.[27]

In other words, Buddhists don't seek out spiritual jobs. Instead, we take the job we already have, and we make it spiritual. Whether we earn a paycheck by sweeping floors or running a business, our livelihood is necessary for our survival in much the same way that farming was necessary for the first Chan Buddhist monks. And like them, we must make our jobs part of our Buddhist practice.

The first way we do this is by ensuring that we earn money in ways that don't cause unnecessary harm to ourselves or others. Of course, no job is perfect in this regard, and we shouldn't expect them to be. A farmer kills countless worms when he plows a field to grow food. And a carpenter must cut down trees if he wants to build a house. However, we can use our inner wisdom to ensure that our profession is causing the least amount of harm possible.

The second way we do this is by being mindful of the benefits we provide humanity through our labor. For example, a housewife provides a comfortable home for her family to enjoy. A teacher educates students so that they can be productive members of society. And a baker provides meals that give people nutrition and comfort.

When we choose a profession that causes a minimal amount of harm (compassion) and we pay attention to how our work assists others (loving-kindness), the result is a feeling of equanimity. Of course, that doesn't mean that we never experience stress while we're working. However, we experience that stress with the understanding that our work, while difficult, makes a difference. And our lives, while imperfect, are useful to the rest of humanity.

Additionally, incorporating our jobs into our spiritual practice helps us feel sympathetic-joy as we go about our daily tasks. An example of this might be a teacher who feels happiness after she helps a struggling student pass a test or a doctor who feels deep satisfaction after her sick patient gets better. As we continue to notice the ways that our jobs help the people around us, we're able to rejoice with them each time they benefit from our labor.

As Westerners, we sometimes believe that our jobs are antithetical to our spiritual practice. But Buddha made Right Livelihood part of the Noble Eightfold Path for a reason. We must work to survive. So, our job must be a central part of our practice, just like it was for our Buddhist ancestors.

**Lesson:** When done correctly, our job is a pathway to enlightenment

## Drawing Water and Carrying Wood

Layman Pang was a Chan Buddhist who lived during the eighth century. He was a wealthy merchant, and his business success allowed him to spend long periods studying sutras and meditating. In fact, at one point, he went so far as to have a small hermitage built on his property because he felt that solitude was an integral part of the practice. Meanwhile, his wife, son, and daughter who were also knowledgeable Dharma practitioners continued living in the house and running the family business.

Late in life, Pang began to worry that his wealth would endanger his spirituality, so he put all of his worldly possessions on a boat, which he promptly sank to the bottom of a deep lake. When asked why he didn't donate his worldly goods to the poor, he wisely responded, "Because I do not want to burden them with my possessions."

After that, Pang went on the road with his family, traveling to various Buddhist monasteries and supporting himself by fashioning bamboo utensils to sell. During this time, he ran into many other travelers who attempted to test his level of attainment. On one occasion, he ran into a student from a rival school who said, "My teacher is so awakened that he can stand on one side of the river, wave a paintbrush in the air, and cause magic symbols to appear on a piece of silk lying on the opposite side of the river. What can you do, old man!"

In his wisdom, Layman Pang listened patiently to the zealous student before giving the following statement:

> *My daily affairs are quite ordinary, but I'm in total harmony with them. I don't hold on to anything, don't reject anything; nowhere an obstacle or conflict. Who cares about wealth and honor? Even the poorest thing shines. My miraculous power and spiritual activity: drawing water and carrying wood.*[28]

There are several lessons that one can take from this exchange. First, it's a commentary on what it means to practice Buddhism. Often, people come to the practice with fanciful ideas of what it means to go on a retreat or realize enlightenment. Like the zealous student, they expect Buddhist practice to involve the attainment of supernatural powers and otherworldly bliss.

It's been my experience that these people are always disappointed. Buddhist retreats involve long stretches of discomfort and boredom. And while there are certainly moments of bliss as we continue along the path, practitioners still experience the same "slings and arrows" of life that non-Buddhists experience.

It's for this reason that Layman Pang offers an alternative view of practice, one rooted in ordinary, everyday life. He uses the phrase "drawing water and carrying wood" to describe this, but that can easily be replaced with "walk the dog and get the newspaper" or "mow the lawn and cook dinner." The key thing to remember is that our spirituality is not separate from our daily activity. Rather, our daily activity is the heart and soul of our spiritual practice.

Second, Pang's commentary tells us a lot about the role of Right Livelihood in Buddhism. It's important to remember that he wasn't a monastic. Rather, he was a lay person with all the duties and responsibilities that go along with that. He had to work to support his family, ensuring that they didn't lack food, water, or a warm place to sleep.

But he doesn't denigrate these activities. Instead, he amplified them by saying, "Even the poorest thing shines." In other words, even the simple act of drawing water and carrying wood so that our family can cook food is worthy of veneration.

Of course, in the modern era, few of us draw water and carry wood anymore. Rather, we have things like electricity and indoor plumbing that provide these things for us. We go to work, earn a paycheck, and pay bills to keep everything running smoothly, but the idea is still the same. As lay people, our livelihood is our spiritual activity. It's a miracle that makes our human existence possible.

**Lesson:** Our daily activities and spiritual practices are the same

# Planting in Straight Lines

When I finished my natural building apprenticeship in Indiana, I traveled to upstate New York, to work as a farming apprentice. The set-up was similar to what I'd done in Indiana; however, instead of doing building and maintenance work, I spent time maintaining a greenhouse, planting an orchard, and working in a strawberry patch.

The woman who owned the farm was named Cindy. She was tall and slender with auburn hair, and she earned income by selling all-natural products (e.g., jam, soap, tea, etc.). Cindy was already growing most of the herbs that she used in her products, and her goal was to start doing the same with many of the fruit varieties that she used. It was a great idea that would improve her profit margins. But clearing land and planting the fruit trees and bushes would require a ton of work. That's where I came in.

On my first day, the Cindy showed me a patch of land that seemed to have been completely forgotten. The perimeter closest to the road was covered in a tangled mass of thorn bushes, and on the other side there was a forest. In between, this metaphorical rock and a hard place there was a patch of land that was covered in rocks and tall grasses. This was where the orchard would go.

My first task was to clear out the briar patch. There was no finesse or special technique involved in doing this. I just took a pair of hedge trimmers and hacked away at the thorn bushes until I had a reasonably large pile of plant parts lying at my feet. Then I dragged what I could to the roadside for trash collection and started the process again. This was difficult work because briars have extremely large thorns, and as they grow, they tend to interlock with another, forming an impenetrable wall of razor-wire that would cut my skin if I wasn't careful. But I persevered, and once the briar patch was cut down, we had easier access to the rest of the property from the roadside.

After that, we set about cutting down the tall grasses where the fruit trees and berry bushes would go. In my experience, most people haven't seen grass in its natural element, when it hasn't been tamed by constant mowing and weed killer treatment. I hadn't seen it until I started work on the orchard.

Each blade of grass was approximately a quarter of an inch wide and roughly three feet tall. It had a coarse texture against my skin, and it grew so thickly that I couldn't see the ground beneath it. Truthfully, it was magnificent to look at, but it was antithetical to the plans we had for the property, so it had to go.

To do this, we borrowed a tractor from a neighbor and hooked a lawn-mowing apparatus to it. Cindy drove the tractor through the field while I ran in front of it and looked for rocks that might damage the mower blades. Anytime, I found one, I'd signal for her to stop. Then I'd carry the offending stone to the edge of the property, and we'd continue mowing.

The locals in upstate New York like to joke that they grow rocks better than anyone else. It's just a reality in that part of the country that no matter how many rocks you remove from your field in the morning, you'll find more in the afternoon. So, between jogging in front of the tractor and carrying an endless number of rocks to the roadside, I got a great work out.

Once that was finished, it was time to begin planting. There were cherry trees that needed to go into the ground along with a seemingly endless number of blueberry and blackberry bushes that would be planted around the outside of the orchard.

We started with the blueberry bushes. Cindy showed me the distance that needed to the left between each plant along with the space that needed to be kept between the rows. After demonstrating the correct way to plant each bush, she went back to the farmhouse to work on some administrative tasks and left me to my own devices.

I worked hard, fighting against a burning sun, heat rash, and a relentless swarm of horse flies. And by the time she came back to pick me up for lunch, a good number of plants were in the ground. Unfortunately, when she walked up to check my work, I could tell that something was wrong.

After standing at the end of a row of blueberry bushes for a few moments, she said, "Come here and tell me what you see." I walked over and looked at the row, but I honestly couldn't see what the problem was. "Look again," Cindy said firmly. As I moved to look from a different angle, she made a motion with her hand that reminded me of a snake slithering through the grass.

As I looked at the row a second time, I saw what she was talking about. I'd been so worried about not planting the bushes too close to one another, that I hadn't ensured that I was planting in a straight line. As a result, the row had a slight S-curve as each plant was either slightly left or right of center.

Thankfully, I wasn't the first know-nothing apprentice that Cindy had dealt with, and she took my error in stride. On the way back to the house, she explained to me why planting crops in a perfectly straight line is so important. If one row is crooked, then that means the one next to it needs to be crooked to compensate. Otherwise, the rows will run perpendicular to one another, and choke points will form where the tractor can't get through without trampling the crops. Multiply this problem by 100 rows, each more crooked than the last, and the result would be utter chaos.

I asked Cindy if she wanted me to re-plant the bushes that were already in the ground, but she said that we'd caught the problem early enough that it wasn't necessary. Instead, we placed extra distance between the crooked row and the second one that I planted to compensate for my error, and I ensured that the second row was ramrod straight. The following rows were made using the second one as a reference point, so there was plenty of room for tractors and farm hands to move between them. I did have to endure some ribbing from time to time about my mistake, but no lasting harm was done.

Looking back, I realize that working in that orchard was a terrific lesson on Right Livelihood. Often, we get so wrapped up in the day-to-day tasks that we lose sight of the big picture. We forget that our work is part of a much larger whole, and our actions have consequences for other people. This is especially true with our jobs, which most people see as simply a way to earn a paycheck.

But there's more to it than that. The work we do enables other people to do their work. And the quality of our work directly affects the quality of their lives. Case in point, the work I did clearing the briar patch allowed Cindy to get the tractor into the field. And the work I did removing rocks made it possible for her to cut the grass without damaging that (expensive) tractor. Finally, the poor job I did planting the first row of blueberry bushes could have made life a lot more challenging down the road for her, and whatever unlucky apprentice came after me.

I say all of this to say that the first step in practicing Right Livelihood is to avoid jobs that cause unnecessary suffering. But the second, equally important step, is to do our jobs well. When we work to the best of our abilities, we make life easier for the people around us. For example, a medical secretary who is diligent in recording incoming calls and scheduling appointments enables the doctors in her office to focus 100 percent on their patients. And a janitor who cleans up spills in the break room ensures that no falls and injures themselves on the wet floor.

This is why the teaching of Right Livelihood is so important to lay Buddhists. It is one of the most effective ways for us to end suffering for ourselves and others. When we show up to work on time, we make life simpler for the person that we're replacing. Now they don't have to work extra to make up for our tardiness, and they get to go home to their families. When we send our boss an update to let him know how our project is going, we're keeping him informed. He has a clear idea of what's happening, and he can make better decisions as a result.

Of course, all these actions are quite ordinary. And there's no guarantee that we'll receive wealth or honor as a result of our actions. But that doesn't stop them from being important. Whether we're running a Fortune 500 company or planting a row of blueberry bushes, the work we do matters. And when we work to the best of our abilities, life gets better for everyone around us.

**Lesson:** Don't underestimate the importance of your work.

# Right Effort

# Sitting on Humpty Dumpty's Wall

My mother used nursery rhymes to teach me how to read. Each night, I'd sit next to her in bed, snug in my footie pajamas. And I'd pick three for us to read together.

First, she'd read the rhyme to me, running her fingers beneath the words so I'd know where we were on the page. Then I'd take the book into my lap and attempt to read it aloud with her helping with the words I didn't know.

As a result, tales of old women who live in shoes and muffin men who live on Drury Lane are etched firmly in my memory. In fact, I've been known to mumble Twinkle Twinkle Little Star to myself when I'm in an especially good mood.

However, a seemingly sad nursery rhyme has been on my mind lately. It's the tale of Humpty Dumpty. Unlike the other rhymes that I read as a child that were either happy or just a bit mischievous in their messages, this one was just tragic. It goes like this:

> *Humpty Dumpty sat on a wall,*
>
> *Humpty Dumpty had a great fall;*
>
> *All the king's horses and all the king's men*
>
> *Couldn't put Humpty together again.*

So, here we have a young man who climbed up on a great wall, probably against his mother's wishes, who proceeded to fall and break every bone in his body. The king's men tried to help him, but he was beyond repair. Thus, Humpty Dumpty was forced to live forever in his humbled, broken state.

I have a lot of questions for whoever thought this story belonged in a children's book. But that's neither here nor there. Instead of dwelling on the past, I'd like to focus on the present and discuss the Buddhist lesson that lies at the heart of this depressing tale.

Often, when people begin Buddhist practice, they do it in response to the suffering in their lives. For example, Dogen became a monk as a result of his mother dying when he was 7. And Shinran practiced Pureland Buddhism because he felt the world was so decrepit that only faith in Amida could save us.

I say all of this to say that people aren't wrong when they come to Buddhism hoping to find relief from suffering. People have been doing exactly that for thousands of years. But we must be cautious with our expectations.

Occasionally, I talk to people who think that if we train hard enough, we'll never be hurt again. Phrases like "final enlightenment" and "mature practice" often get thrown around in these discussions. But this thinking is incorrect.

Because each of us lives as Humpty Dumpty, perched precariously on a great wall. We struggle to carry our baggage (jobs, families, bills, etc.) throughout the day. But sometimes our burden is too heavy. Sometimes we fall headfirst toward the concrete pavement below.

And as we lie there broken and bleeding on the ground, conventional society tries to save us. The TV tries to distract us. Food tries to comfort us. And pets try to drown our sorrow with kisses. But it's all for naught. All the king's horses and all the king's men can't put us together again. That's what the Dharma is for.

Because the promise of Buddhism is not that we'll never be broken; rather, it's a promise that states we'll never *stay* broken. No matter how many times we tumble from the wall, our practice will always be there, piecing us back together, and sending us on our way.

Over time, the practice makes us stronger, more resilient. We learn what pieces of baggage aren't worth carrying, gladly throwing them away. And we get better at carrying the things that are left. Eventually, we lose our fear of falling, not because it doesn't hurt, but because we know we'll get back up again.

**Lesson:** Don't be afraid to fall

## Shojin Ryori

In Japanese Buddhism, Shojin is a word used to denote elevation of the soul through intense focus on a single task. It's most often used to describe the ritualized cooking of vegetarian meals in Buddhist temples, known as Shojin Ryori.

During the preparation of Shojin Ryori cuisine, monks go to the market and *greet* their vegetables. First, they smell each one individually. Then they use their fingers to massage the plant and investigate its texture. After that, they return home and slowly chop each one by hand. Nothing is wasted.

The use of machines (including refrigerators) is frowned upon in Shojin Ryori, so cooks buy only as much as they need for a meal and utilize every part of the plant.

They spend hours grinding spices with a pestle and mortar. And then they create a dish that carefully balances the colors, textures, and flavor profiles of every ingredient. The result is that the mundane task of cooking vegetables becomes a work of art. But more than that, it becomes a lesson in how beautiful life can be when we put our whole heart into the present moment.

"Just stir the pot," the Shojin teacher says. "Just chop the vegetables. Just serve the food. Do it over and over again. Do it until your mind explodes. Do it until the training takes away every hope, dream, and desire that you have. Do it until you realize that 'this' is all you have in life. And then learn to cherish this — whatever it might be.

Cherish the pot, cherish the vegetables, cherish the long commute and the annoying relatives. Cherish your boring, everyday life, and appreciate how lucky you are to have it."

This is an important lesson for anyone who chooses to walk the Buddhist path. It's tempting to think that our ordinary lives are a hindrance to spiritual practice, that any time not spent meditating is a waste. But what is Buddhism if not training in how to live our normal lives wholeheartedly?

What is meditation if not the stripping away of every trick, technique, and piece of technology that we use to escape this present moment?

Sadly, it's easy to fall into the trap of thinking that *living in the moment* is preparation for something else. We wait with bated breath for the lesson that will be revealed by washing dishes. We watch sunsets in the hope that we'll feel something special. In short, we think that if we can learn to be ordinary enough, then something extraordinary will happen.

But if Shojin teaches us anything, it's that washing dishes is the lesson, and the sunset is already special. But we don't realize that because we're not paying attention. We're so wrapped up in our search for something better that we miss out on the perfection of the here and now.

That's why the Buddhist practice of Shojin Ryori is so powerful. It strips away any hint of glamour or mystique that could be attached to spiritual practice.

The monks use plain rice and ordinary vegetables in their cooking. They prepare food using age-old techniques that require countless hours of chopping vegetables and grinding spices. They stand over hot stoves and pay attention to the minutest details in their food presentation (color, texture, symmetry, etc.) until their intense devotion to the ordinary task of cooking bears extraordinary and tasty food.

In this way, Shojin Ryori practitioners can turn vegetarian cooking into a pathway toward awakening. And we can do the same by simply living every day with a full heart. When we practice Shojin, we go to work, we pay our bills, we cook our food, and enlightenment takes care of itself.

# Pulling Weeds and Planting Strawberries

One of my duties when I worked as a farm apprentice in upstate New York, was to tend a strawberry patch. I'd been eating strawberries my whole life, but I had no idea what went into growing them. So, this work ended up being a terrific learning opportunity for me. And I learned a lot about farming and Buddhism in the process.

For example, I was under the impression that farmers always grow their plants from seed. However, this isn't always the case. With strawberries, most varieties require a year to get established and start bearing fruit. So, many farmers will either start the seedlings off in a controlled environment like a greenhouse before planting them outdoors or they will order them online.

Once the plants are in the ground, weeds become a major issue. Strawberries grow close to the ground, so they can easily get crowded out by weeds if the farmer isn't careful. To control for this, farmers place black plastic over the seed beds and punch holes in it at regular intervals where the strawberries are planted.

Unfortunately, weeds are incredibly resilient, and over time, they will grow in the small space between the strawberry plant and the plastic. That's where I came in. Many of the old seed beds had weeds growing up around the strawberry plants. Additionally, there were new beds that had been prepared the year before, but the plastic covering hadn't been placed over them yet.

So, my job was two-fold. In the established beds, I had to pull the weeds from around the plants, being careful not to damage the strawberry or tear the plastic. In the new beds, I had to pull all the large weeds that had grown up since the previous year and till the soil with a steel rake and a garden hoe. When that was done, the planting bed was covered with black plastic, and I commenced to punching holes in the appropriate places and planting strawberries.

I remember feeling discouraged the first time I looked at one of the beds and started thinking about how much work lay ahead of me. In some places, there were so many weeds that you couldn't even see the strawberries! But I'd been given a job to do, and the only option I had was to put my head down and get to work.

At first, I would occasionally stop to look up from my work and check to see how much farther I had to go. But this just made the task seem even more difficult, and I never felt like I was making enough progress. So, I quickly made up my mind that I wouldn't look at the end of the row or try to gauge how much work I had left to do. Instead, I focused solely on the strawberry plant that was in front of me.

I'm sure I looked silly to anyone who drove past as I walked all over the fields with my head aimed at the ground, but my method worked. The more I focused solely on the task in front of me as opposed to the work that was waiting for me in the future, the more manageable the job became. And as I did that over and over again, pulling one clump of weeds after another, I inevitably reached the end of the planting bed.

This was always the best part, when I could look over my work and see all of the planted strawberries that now had plenty of room to grow. Sometimes, I even took before and after pictures on my phone to commemorate the event!

In many ways, the practice of Right Effort is a lot like tending a strawberry patch. If we think of our mind as a garden, then each of us has a host of weeds (unwholesome qualities) that have grown within us over time. Of course, we shouldn't feel ashamed of this fact. It's perfectly natural for weeds to grow when a garden is not tended. Thankfully, the Dharma gives us step-by-step instructions on how to pull our weeds out by the roots, creating the conditions for strawberries (wholesome qualities) to grow.

However, there are no shortcuts on the path. And if we waste time checking our progress, we'll become discouraged. That's why it's so important to keep our heads down and focus solely on what's in front of us. We don't need to remove all of the greed, anger, and ignorance from our lives. We just need to remove the greed, anger, and ignorance that we feel in this present moment. We don't need to meditate every day. We just need to meditate today.

If we take this approach to practice, putting our efforts into cultivating our mind-gardens in this present moment, it's inevitable that we'll realize enlightenment. But we must be willing to put in the work. If we do this, we'll have plenty of strawberries to eat as we walk the Buddhist path.

**Lesson:** There are no shortcuts when tending the mind-garden

## The Three-Fold Path of Right Effort

When Buddhists think of Right Effort, they normally think in terms of hard work and dedication. Thus, the teaching becomes a willingness to show a strong commitment to one's practice. This is 100 percent correct. We can't get anywhere in Buddhism or life if we aren't willing to exert ourselves. However, there is a second part of the teaching that can't be ignored.

In addition to having a strong commitment to practice, we must ensure that we are using our energy in appropriate ways. That is to say, we must ensure that we are doing actions that help us realize awakening and avoiding actions that don't.

However, it should be noted that this isn't a one-time act. We don't recite a single sutra or sit a single retreat, and then we're set for life. Rather, it is a continuous process that results in our getting a little better each day.

If we forget this seemingly simple fact, it's very easy to become discouraged in our practice. For example, I struggled for a long time with the fact that I could sit for meditation in the morning and feel like my mind was free of any negative qualities only to find myself feeling sadness or anger by the end of my workday. On the surface, it seemed like I hadn't accomplished anything and that my practice was inconsequential. But a closer inspection revealed something very different.

While it was true that I still experienced unwholesome mental qualities after meditation, it was also true that I was less beholden to them. In other words, when I felt anger, I noticed it and tried to come up with a healthy response instead of simply lashing out. Sometimes, this manifested in my waiting until I calmed down before sending an email so that I could communicate using Right Speech. Other times, it involved my taking a day to mull over a problem so that I could respond with Right Action. But in each case, the goal wasn't to never feel negative emotions again. Rather, the goal was to ensure that I responded appropriately, in a way that didn't make those emotions worse.

Additionally, I found that I was putting more effort into avoiding places and situations that caused negative mind states to arise. For example, I found that a lot of the anger and misunderstandings that happened in my friend circle traced back to alcohol. People (myself included) would get drunk and say or do things without thinking that resulted in hurt feelings. As a response to this, I stopped drinking alcohol. Thus, I was able to avoid a lot of that drama.

Of course, we can't only focus on the negative. Right Effort also requires us to cultivate positive mental states. Thankfully, Buddhism provides us with many methods for doing that in our daily life. For example, meditation is a good way to develop equanimity, generosity helps us feel sympathetic-joy, and chanting can help us feel loving-kindness toward the people around us. When we generate energy and exert our minds toward these practices, it becomes easier for us to walk peacefully in the world. And we develop the spiritual reserves necessary to deal with negative mind states when they arise.

Additionally, we may find other practices that we don't associate with Buddhism, which help us to cultivate positive qualities. Making a point to share a meal with family could help us feel more compassion toward them. And doing volunteer work is another great way to develop a mind of generosity.

So, there are three major parts to the teaching of Right Effort, which go as follows:

1. We must show a strong commitment to practice and be willing to devote time and energy to our training.

2. We must show a strong commitment to eliminating unwholesome mind states, avoiding things that cause them to arise, and striving to deal with them appropriately when they do.

3. We must show a strong commitment to developing wholesome mind states, seeking out things that cause them to arise, and engaging in practices that help us cultivate them.

As we engage in these three practices, our minds naturally become calmer and more peaceful. Over time, they just become a natural part of our daily lives, and we don't even realize what we're doing. But it must be remembered that the practice of Right Effort is a constant, ongoing thing. In the words of Rev. Koyo Kubose, "There arc no periods in Buddhism. We just keep going"

**Lesson:** Find the path, walk thc path, and you'll eventually get where you're going.

## The Five Hindrances

As human beings, we sometimes falter when we walk the Buddhist path. We have the best of intentions, hoping against hope to end suffering for ourselves and other sentient beings. But inevitably, obstacles arise that make it difficult for us to walk the path. This is especially true when it comes to the practice of Right Effort.

We might have a strong desire to meditate when we get home, but then a favorite TV show comes on, and we forget. Or wc may drive to work with the intention of treating all living beings with compassion, but then a semi-truck almost runs us off the road. There are a host of problems that keep us from practicing the Dharma. And we can become discouraged if we don't learn how to deal with them effectively.

But none of these issues are new. For as long as Buddhism has existed, there have been people who struggled to make the practice part of their daily lives. However, in his wisdom, Buddha divided the major hinderances to Right Effort into five categories:

1. Sensual Desire
2. Ill Will
3. Sloth and Drowsiness
4. Restlessness and Anxiety
5. Doubt[29]

Learning to deal with these hindrances effectively is a key component of Right Effort. And while it's not always easy, it's simple to counter each one of them. The key is to pay close attention to our body, speech, and mind in every moment so that we aren't caught by surprise when hindrances to practice arise. When we do this, we can stop them in their tracks, and exert the necessary energy to continue our training. Some of the ways that I deal with the five hindrances are as follows:

**Sensual Desire -** The truth is that sometimes we don't want to practice. This can happen if we're overloaded with work, or we've made plans to go out with friends. I deal with this hindrance in two ways.

First, I work to integrate my practice into everyday activities. For example, I often chant nembutsu while I'm riding in elevators, and I practice mindfulness of the body while walking; focusing on the feeling of the pavement against my feet. That way, there's no conflict between my practice and daily life.

Second, if I find myself short on time, I'll abbreviate my meditation instead of abandoning it altogether. So, if I don't have time to meditate for an hour, I'll meditate for 30 minutes.

**Ill Will -** If we aren't careful, feelings of aversion that we have toward people or objects can keep us from practicing with the right amount of vigor. It's difficult to sit on the cushion when our minds are filled with anger.

One of the ways I counter this is by reminding myself that Buddhist practice helps neutralize feelings of ill will. In other words, if I'm trapped in the mind of anger, I take that as a sign that I need to practice more, not less! In this way, the ill will becomes a source of motivation as opposed to being a hindrance.

Additionally, I strive to avoid actions that stoke the fires of my ill will. So, if I'm angry at someone, I'll avoid speaking negatively about them to another person. Instead, I'll make a point of speaking about the kindness and generosity that they've shown me in the past.

**Sloth and Drowsiness -** Tiredness can play a big role in our inability to practice. The world can take a lot out of us, and during these moments, Buddhist practice may seem like one in a long list of items on our to-do list that's sapping our strength.

When I find that a feeling of sloth or drowsiness is getting in the way of my practice, I always check to ensure that I'm getting enough sleep. If not, I work to prioritize being well-rested for my morning sit over whatever movie or TV show I may want to watch in the evening.

Also, when I'm feeling too tired to practice, I motivate myself by remembering that this isn't just about me. The Dharma is a gift that I give both to myself and all sentient beings. Thus, I may not be able to do something directly about the terrible things I see on the news. But I can ensure that I go into the world with a pure mind that will allow me to help where I can.

**Restlessness and Anxiety** - Between social media, cell phones, and the 24-hour news cycle, restlessness and anxiety have become constant companions for many of us. It always seems like there's one more thing that we need to get done before we can sit down and study a sutra or chant.

When I start to feel this way, I bring my attention to the present moment by practicing mindfulness of the breath. This involves closing my eyes and placing all of my attention on the feeling of air entering my nostrils along with the expansion and contraction of my rib cage with each breath of air. Doing this helps to change my mind-state so that I'm able to focus fully on practice.

Additionally, I remind myself that I'm not ignoring the other things in my life when I take time out of my day for training. Rather, I'm preparing myself to deal with those things more effectively.

**Uncertainty** - No matter how dedicated we are to walking the Buddhist path, we will experience doubt from time to time. We may wonder if the practice is worth it, or if we're truly capable of realizing enlightenment.

I've found that the greatest antidote to uncertainty is faith. First, we must have faith in ourselves and our inherent enlightenment. We must remember that Buddha was a human being just like us, and he was able to walk the path successfully. There's no reason we can't do it as well.

Second, we must have faith in the practice. Some parts of it may seem strange to us, and others may be harder than we would like, but it's been around for well over 2,600 years. And it wouldn't have lasted that long if it didn't do what it promised. So, we can trust it in the same way that we might trust an old friend who we've known since grade school.

I've also found that practicing with other Buddhists can be helpful. When we have questions or doubts about our practice, speaking with Dharma friends or a trusted teacher can help lay our fears to rest.

The five hindrances have been a thorn in the side of Buddhists going back to the time of the Buddha. However, they're not something to be feared. Rather, we must accept them in the same way that we accept unpleasant weather and exert ourselves to deal with them effectively. When we do this, the entire world opens to us, and our practice grows stronger as a result.

Lesson: Right Effort turns our hindrances into helpers on the path.

# Right Mindfulness

# Naikan

Naikan is a mindfulness and self-reflection practice that was created by a Japanese Buddhist named Yoshimoto Ishin. He created the practice as an alternative to the ascetic contrition practice, Mishirabe, which involves sensory deprivation and abstaining from food, water, and sleep. A devout Jodo Shinshu practitioner, Ishin performed Mishirabe as a young man, but he created Naikan so that people would have a simpler way to study themselves and their relationships.[30]

The practice can be done for varying lengths of time, ranging from several days to several weeks, and it requires students to reflect on three questions and take note of their responses. The questions are as follows:

- What have I received today?
- What have I given today?
- What troubles and difficulties have I caused others?

The first two questions are extremely powerful because human beings are born with a negativity bias. That is to say, we naturally pay more attention to the sad, hurtful parts of life. As a result, it's easy for us to miss the variety of gifts that we give and receive each day.

Naikan helps us counter our negativity bias by providing a structured method for noticing the blessings in our life. For example, we might answer the first question by saying, "My employer gave me a paycheck," or "My spouse took out the garbage." Ordinarily, we might take these things for granted, but the practice requires us to take note of them. When we do this, we may reflect on how difficult life would be if we didn't have a paycheck or our house was filled with garbage.

Our answers to the second question work similarly; perhaps we gave a co-worker some much-needed advice on a project, or we shared a meal with a friend. Again, our initial tendency may be to chalk these things up as "no big deal." But the reality is that these simple acts made life appreciably better for the other person. When we answer the second question, we may reflect on the many ways we help others throughout the day without realizing it.

The third question serves as a sort of gut check, helping us keep track of things that we can do differently in the future. For example, maybe we were short with our kids when they asked for help with a homework assignment. In this case, we'd take note of our mistake and work to be more careful in the future.

My first exposure to Naikan was in 2016 when I was a lay ministry student in the Bright Dawn Center of Oneness Buddhism. As part of our training, we were required to read *Naikan: Gratitude, Grace and the Japanese Art of Self-Reflection* by Gregg Krech. We also had to keep a Naikan journal for 30 days and participate in weekly discussions about our experiences.

During this time, I pulled out my journal every night and wrote down five things that I received that day, five things that I gave to others, and one way in which I'd caused trouble for other people. We were instructed to use the 5-5-1 ratio to avoid dwelling on negativity.

As I engaged with the practice, I learned not to be so enthralled by my mind. I realized that I wasn't a passive observer, and I had a choice in what experiences I wanted to focus on in the same way that I had a choice in what I wanted to look at when walking down the street. A stroll to the local bodega could be pleasant or unpleasant, depending on whether I focused on the garbage lying in the street or the birds singing in the trees. Similarly, the world seemed like a lonely place when my inner dialogue rattled off all of the things that I lacked at the moment.

But when I intentionally sat down and answered the question "What have I been given," I realized that I was being cared for in myriad ways. The sun gave me warmth, my landlord provided me with indoor plumbing, and the clerk smiled at me when they rang up my groceries. Who could ask for more?

In contrast, the third question "What troubles and difficulties have I caused others?" helped me see that I wasn't always the innocent victim. There were times when I inadvertently said or did things that caused confrontations or made them worse. Through Naikan practice, I learned to identify these moments and found ways to do better in the future.

Each of us exists in the universe, both giving and receiving help from others through the day. Yes, we make mistakes and occasionally cause trouble, but this, too, is part of life's natural ebb and flow. Naikan practice helps us to see this flow more clearly and see the positive interactions that exist in every moment of every day.

**Lesson:** Mindfulness helps us see the world clearly and reflect on the give and take of life

# A Walk in the Garden

I've always had a fascination with the Pacific Northwest. Between college trips, the Marine Corps, and months-long trips to find myself, I've been fortunate to see many different parts of the world. But for some reason, my traveling shoes haven't taken me to that corner of the world very often. I think that's why it's so alluring. We always have the deepest longing for the things we can't have.

So, I packed my bags in the summer of 2017, and I jumped on a train heading west. At this point, my savings were built up to a semi-respectable level, and I had PTO (paid-time-off) to burn, so I decided to fulfill my dreams of seeing what the Pacific Northwest had to offer. When I was farming, I'd met many travelers who had either come from Portland, Oregon, or they were heading in that direction. So, I chose that as my destination.

When I arrived in the city, it was amid a heatwave. While I was there, the temperature never went below 90 degrees and a couple of days broke 100. More surprising than the weather, however, were the people. I've always felt that cities are living organisms with personalities all their own. And you can learn about that personality through the people who live there. Chicagoans are hard-nosed and gritty. New Yorkers are always in a hurry. And Portlanders… Portlanders are weird in all the best ways.

Case in point: I walked into a bar called LikeWise in SE Portland one night, and I was shocked to learn that there were more than drinks on the menu. The establishment also sold experiences. For example, if you paid $300, the bartender would close the bar for two hours and take you to a local house to share a six-pack. Or you could pay $700, and the bar owners would close for the day and drive you to the coast for a seafood dinner.[31]

Not wanting to spend all of my travel money in one place I opted to pay $30 in exchange for a non-alcoholic drink and a page torn out of a random book they had on the shelf. The bartender ended up selecting a book called *Grape Fruit*, written by Yoko Ono. And my torn-out page included missives such as,

> *Give death announcements each time you move instead of giving announcements of the change of address. Send the same when you die.[32]*

I still carry that slip of paper in my wallet to this day. It makes for a great conversation piece at parties. But Portland wasn't just good for fun, head-scratching experiences. I also got to experience some culture as well. The pinnacle of which was when I visited the Lan Su Chinese garden, which is a botanical garden located in NW Portland. It was designed to mirror traditional Ming Dynasty gardens, blending art, architecture, and nature.[33]

The best part of walking through the garden was seeing the drastic changes that occurred as we moved from one area to the next. One moment, the ground would be perfectly smooth, and in the next, it would be hard and bumpy. Standing in one spot gave me a perfect view of a pond and abundant plant life. But standing in another spot a few feet away left me staring at four stone walls with nothing visible but the sky.

The tour guide explained that this was done on purpose so that the garden would present a different "picture" to its inhabitants depending on where they stood. Textures, architecture, and even smells changed from one place to the next so that I was forced to use all of my senses. I smelled tea coming from the tea house, I felt pebbles through my shoes, and I saw the water rippling beneath the bridge that connected one half of the garden to the other.

The tour guide also explained that it was impossible to fully experience the garden in one visit. Sure, I could walk all of the paths in a day. But that only showed me what it was like in the sunshine. I'd have to walk it again at night. And that would be a good start, but I'd still need to experience it in the rain, and in the snow, and as an old man.

In short, the garden was a living thing. It grew and changed with each passing moment. I could walk in it for a hundred years, and never experience the whole thing.

In many ways, human life is a lot like the Lan Su garden. It's a living thing. That may seem like a foolish and obvious statement. But many of us don't treat each day as if it were alive. Rather, we walk the well-worn paths to our cars, our jobs, and our family dinners with the expectation that not much has changed. As a result, we miss out on the nuanced beauty of our lives.

But Right Mindfulness ensures that we don't miss a thing. It helps us engage with life more fully. And as we pay attention to our body, mind, emotions, and mental objects, we experience the world differently. We notice the feel of the carpet against our feet, and we savor the taste of our food during meals. We go about our daily tasks as if they were brand new. And we honor the emotions that arise with each one.

As we continue to walk mindfully in the garden of our lives, we see things more clearly. We understand that the "picture" of our life differs depending on where we choose to stand. So, we stand in places that give us the most light. We determine which paths lead to suffering, and we instinctively learn to avoid them. More than that, we recognize the ever-changing, unexpected nature of our existence. And we pay close attention to each moment as a result.

Sometimes, this practice leads us to a bar that hands out reading material. Other times, we meet a tour guide who gives us life-changing advice. The practice can manifest in many ways, but one thing is always true. We can walk the same path 1,000 times, and still find something new.

**Lesson:** Mindfulness helps us find joy in both the routine and the unexpected

## Mindful Social Media

Social networking sites are becoming an integral part of daily life for many of us. In the beginning, they were strictly for entertainment. However, in recent years, they've become a marketing platform for big business, a way for politicians to reach voters, and the primary form of communication for family and friends. All of this is fine in and of itself. After all, radio and television were equally disruptive when in their early days. And we all turned out fine. But there is a down-side.

As our lives become increasingly engulfed by Facebook groups and Twitter pages, we can lose sight of reality. In fact, heavy social media usage has been linked to depression; resulting from participants feeling unpopular or unsuccessful due to the posts they see online.[34] More than that, feelings of isolation can occur as people look to the internet for the validation and close relationships that would normally come from family members and co-workers.

As a result, we must be very careful in how we use these technologies, ensuring that they become a tool for our benefit and not our reason for existence. Mindfulness can help us do this by revealing our motivations for posting online and helping us see when thing things are getting out of hand.

The following guidelines are methods that I use in my personal life to mindfully use social media.

## Log-Out When You're Finished

Many social networking sites use cookies to track our usage. This allows them to show us ads that they think we'll like and change our timeline in ways that we'll enjoy. For example, someone who watches lots of cat videos on YouTube will see recommendations for other cat videos.

Additionally, cookies make it, so we don't have to log-in every time we want to visit a site. In fact, if we use them regularly from the same devices, some social networking sites will allow users to go weeks or even months without verifying their password.

Of course, this is very convenient. But it causes us to be extremely mindless in our usage. If we don't need to log in or out of a site, then we never have to question why we're using it. Instead, we open it up whenever we have a free moment, turning our back on the real world in favor of the virtual one.

To counteract this, we must log-out of social networking sites once we finish browsing. The extra time it takes for us to log back in later will give us a necessary pause so that we can investigate why we want to use the site.

**Ask Yourself "Why"**

Before we log-in to a social networking site, it's important to investigate the feelings that have brought us there. Do we have a specific task that we're trying to accomplish like sending out a birthday invite, or are we trying to escape feelings of insecurity or boredom? If our answer leans more toward the latter, it may be helpful to simply sit with those emotions and allow ourselves to process them without distraction.

Also, we must investigate our feelings before posting something on the internet, asking ourselves why we're doing it. For example, if we're feeling angry, our first inclination may be to post a hurtful message. However, anger is listed as one of the Three Poisons for a reason. And any post that's rooted in anger is guaranteed to cause suffering for ourselves and others.

If we find that our post is rooted in greed, anger, or ignorance, then it may be a good idea not to post it. Or if the post is rooted in feelings of sadness or grief, turning to our real-world counterparts (family, friends, therapists, etc.) may be more helpful in terms of working through our pain.

**Don't Get Caught Up in the Illusion**

The sutras warn us about the dangers of getting caught up in the phenomenal world, and nowhere is this more apparent on the internet. Advertisements are designed to stimulate us in just the right ways to make us buy. And social media influencers present unrealistic versions of life that tell us that we're only one diet, vacation, or make-up tutorial from perfection.

All of this works to stimulate the mind of desire, which is the root of all suffering. To counteract this, we must engage with social media in the same way that we engage with cartoons. We can watch what people post and enjoy what we're seeing, but we must be careful not to take any of it seriously.

**Get Physical**

In terms of communication or life experiences, social media should be our last resort. It's great to look at pictures of a beautiful hiking trail, but it's better for both our bodies and our spirit if we go out and hike the trail ourselves.

Similarly, there's nothing wrong with speaking to friends and loved ones via social media. But other communication methods are better if we want an embodied experience. That is to say; a phone call is much better than a text message or wall post. And an in-person visit is even better than that.

Sure, posting pictures of your vacation online is a good way to get the word out. But inviting our friends over so that we can share them in-person allows for a more embodied experience and leads to stronger relationships. When it comes to communication, the more physical we can get, the better.

Social media is here to stay whether we like it, or not. And while some people have been successful in simply unplugging from this medium, many of us have job requirements and social pressures that require us to be online. As a result, we must work hard to find ways to mindful and not mindless in how we use these mediums.

If we force ourselves to log out after each session, investigate our feelings as we browse our timelines, and remember to interact with the world physically, then social media can be a tool that enriches our lives.

**Lesson:** Be mindful, not mindless when you use social media


# Perfectly Ordinary

On December 8 of each year Buddhists all over the world celebrate Bodhi day, which commemorates the day that Buddha realized enlightenment. The celebrations take many forms ranging from festive parties complete with rich food and music, to somber ceremonies with lots of chanting and meditation.

In December 2017, I celebrated Bodhi day by participating in a three-day retreat that was led by Ven. Shih Ying-Fa and the other monks of the Nien-Fo Chan order. A cabin was rented from what used to be a Christian summer camp and approximately 20 people including myself crowded inside to practice. To maintain a contemplative atmosphere, several rules were handed down at the beginning of the practice period.

The use of cell phones and laptops were strictly forbidden. And we were encouraged to maintain noble silence whenever possible. Additionally, we were encouraged to refrain from making eye contact with the other participants. This is all standard for a meditation retreat. The goal is to create an environment where the student has no choice but to turn inward and study their minds. And the rules serve to eliminate distractions.

The practice included seated meditation, chanting, Zen dialogues where we could discuss our practice 1:1 with Ven. Ying Fa, and outdoor walking meditation. As with any long period of silence and introspection, there were many "ah-ha" moments that rocked me to my core. I learned more about myself, my relationships, and how I want to live in the world than I could ever put into a single book. However, there were two lessons that I found especially helpful.

The first came during food services. Meals were eaten in a group setting with three - four people sitting at each table. The monks laid food at each table buffet-style, and it was up to the retreatants to divvy up the meal amongst themselves. I should stop here and say that I love to eat, and I'm almost always snacking on something. In fact, my co-workers joke that they can always find me at work by following the smell of food.

That being said, I was surprised by the strong emotions that came up during meals. Here I was, sitting at a table brimming with delicious food, and whether I got something to eat or not was entirely in the hands of other people. For example, there was nothing to stop a hungry retreatant from plopping all the rice on their plate, leaving the rest of us with nothing.

On the flip side, when it was my turn to serve myself, I had the responsibility of both making sure that I gave myself a reasonable portion and ensuring that there was something left for the next person. So, each time we sat down to eat. I experienced being both powerful and powerless in the span of a few minutes. Experiencing this ebb and flow was valuable because it forced me to be intentional with my decisions.

Was I taking this extra scoop of vegetables because I was hungry and in need of nourishment, or was my fear of missing out causing me to be greedy? Did I leave enough food for the next person, and how could I know since we weren't allowed to talk?

Questions like these ran through my mind each time I sat down to a meal, requiring me to be mindful of my emotions, my body, and the needs of the people around me. In short, I had to pay close attention during every meal to ensure that everyone (including myself) got enough to eat. And in the end, I landed on a simple solution.

The first-time food was passed around, I made a point of taking a little bit less than I wanted to ensure there was enough to go around. When everyone had received their portion, I would point at each serving bowl and look at my table mates. If they grabbed the bowl and got more food, then I felt sympathetic joy knowing that they got their fill. If they shook their head as if to say, "no," then I got seconds, secure in the fact that no one was going without.

We all practice this sort of dance in daily life. There are moments when we're sitting at the head of the table, calling the shots. And there are others when we're stuck in line at the supermarket with 20 people ahead of us. And as we alternate between feeling powerful and feeling powerless mindfulness helps us navigate what's happening.

In moments when we're in control, we must be mindful of others, ensuring that we don't deprive them of the things they need. In contrast, when we're not in control, we must be mindful of our own needs and find ways to advocate for ourselves respectfully. When we do this, we create a world where everyone gets what they need, even if they don't get what they want.

The second lesson came during one of our outdoor walking meditations. Walking meditation is a standard part of the practice at many Buddhist temples. It can be done in many ways, but it generally consists of participants walking in single file around the perimeter of a room or in a pre-set course outdoors. This allows them to stretch their legs and get some much-needed exercise after long periods of sitting. It also teaches them how to maintain a peaceful mind-state in daily life as they strive to walk and meditate at the same time.

During the meditation, I was following behind the person in front of me and practicing mindfulness of the body. More specifically, I was focusing on the feeling of air moving in and out of my lungs along with the feeling of the ground beneath my shoes. This was effective in terms of keeping me in the present moment, but sometimes I'd get too wrapped up in the practice and start to fall behind.

So, I switched and started focusing on my surrounding. Every few steps I would pick an object (e.g., a stone, a tree, a leaf) and watch it closely as I walked. When I finally moved past it, I would pick another object and focus on that. After a couple of loops, I began picking specific stones, trees, and leaves to focus on depending where we were on the path. Each time I strove to see a little more detail in them than I did before.

At one point, I looked down at the ground for a specific leaf that I'd chosen as one of my objects of focus. When I found it, the person in front of me stepped on it, and when they removed their foot, it felt like a switch had been turned on in my head. It was as if I'd been watching a movie on a black and white cathode TV from the '60s one moment, and in the next, I was watching that same movie on a super High Definition TV from the modern era.

When I looked at the leaf, I could see every wrinkle and vein on its surface. And I was confused as to how I hadn't seen them before. Next, I looked at a tree several feet away that marked the point where we'd turn around to start heading back toward the cabin. I marveled at how the bark of the tree wasn't just brown anymore; it was BROWN. It felt like I saw the essence of the color itself. More than that, I noticed that the tree wasn't just one shade. There were multiple hues of brown living within its branches like one of those color-matching pallets that can be found at a hardware store.

I imagined a store clerk describing each one in detail as I walked, "This particular branch starts as a taupe color near the tree trunk before darkening to a brilliant umber at its tip…" It was a lovely experience, but it was overwhelming. And when we got back to the cabin, I was relieved that the world returned to its original, muted tones as soon as I stepped through the door.

We spent the next several hours chanting, eating, and practicing seated meditation, and the time came for us to do another outdoor walk. This time, when we stepped outside, everything was exactly as it had always been. The trees appeared as a single shade of brown. The dead leaves were unremarkable. And I was thoroughly disappointed. To be sure, I'd been taken aback by the high-resolution view of the world that I'd experienced earlier. But there was a specialness about it. It had felt like I was seeing some secret corner of the earth for the first time, and now I was back in the uninspired realm of the ordinary.

I chewed on this for a while as we walked. Then on a whim, I grabbed a leaf off the ground and held it a few inches from my face. To my surprise, the wrinkles, veins, and valleys that I'd seen in it previously were still there. I just had to look more closely to see them. Next, I stepped off the trail and stared intently at a nearby tree. Sure enough, at this distance, I could see that it wasn't a single shade of brown. Rather, there was a veritable rainbow emanating from its bark with colors ranging from coffee to near black.

Thus, I realized that the world hadn't changed between the morning walk and this one. Rather, it was my mind that changed. All the beauty and brilliance that I'd seen earlier in the day was still here, but I couldn't be passive if I wanted to see it. Rather, I had to exert effort and be mindful of the world around me. I had to look closely at the leaves, the trees, and the gravel on the road if I wanted to see the treasures therein. Anything less would leave me with a false, one-dimensional view of the world.

Of course, this doesn't just apply to walks in the woods. Each day, we make a choice around if we want to see the low-res or the high-res version of the world. And the difference between the two isn't a series of magic words or a special password. It's mindfulness. It's our willingness (or lack thereof) to give the world our full attention.

Mindfulness shifts our thinking so that a simple meal transforms into a gift from all sentient beings. It helps us appreciate the joy that comes from a favorite chair. And it reminds us to look out for our neighbor. It allows us to see the beauty and intricate details of the trees, leaves, people, and things around us, remaking an ordinary world into a perfectly ordinary one.

**Lesson:** Mindfulness helps us see perfection in the ordinary

## Mindfulness and Toilet Gassho

If I had to sum up the teaching of Right Mindfulness succinctly, I would call it, "Paying Attention." More specifically, Right Mindfulness requires us to pay attention to four facets of our existence that impact both the quality of our practice and our ability to walk the path. These facets are:

- Mind - This relates to mental states that we experience (calmness, sleepiness, peace, etc.)
- Body - The describes our physical body as it exists in the world
- Feelings - This denotes our emotions (anger, joy, fear, etc.)
- Mental Objects - These are conceptual ideas we have about the world around us

When we place our full attention on these things, it becomes easier to break negative mental habits. For example, there is a Vipassana practice called "labeling" that helps practitioners do this by instructing them to give a one-word label to anything that they may be experiencing in the moment. If they are feeling anger, they think the word "anger" without engaging with the emotion beyond that single word.[35]

Doing this creates space between the practitioner and their emotion and allows them to respond differently than they would if they allowed the anger to consume them.

Similarly, mindfulness of the body can be useful if we're having trouble focusing on the present moment. We do this by paying attention to the sensations on the bottom of our feet as we walk or the feeling of air in our lungs as we breathe. As we pay attention to these things, thoughts about the past and future fall away as we become more attuned to the physical nature of this present moment.

In my own life, mindfulness became an instrumental part of my practice in the spring of 2015, when I decided to hang up my farming boots and return to a conventional lifestyle. Initially, I'd decided to live and work on organic farms because I thought that lifestyle was more spiritual than my regular office job.

And while the eight months that I spent traveling allowed me to spend several hours each day in meditation along with teaching me valuable life skills, it also showed me that there is no escape from the real world. In fact, many of the problems that I'd been trying to escape (greed, favoritism, difficulty in balancing spiritual and work responsibilities, etc.) existed on every farm I visited.

So, I used what was left of my meager savings to buy a shirt and tie, and I went back to working in a cubicle. But it wasn't a smooth transition, and I spent a lot of time wondering if I could be a good Buddhist and still work with computers all day.

I received my answer when I began practicing in the Bright Dawn Center of Oneness Buddhism, where I was taught that there's no separation between the spiritual world and the conventional one. Traditionally, Pure Land Buddhism teaches that the world is so impure that we have no hope of realizing enlightenment in this ordinary plane of existence.

So, we must strive to purify ourselves through visualization and recitation of the Buddha's name so that we can be reborn in a pure land after death.[36] In this Buddhist pure land, we'll then find the perfect conditions for us to realize enlightenment. However, Reverend Gyomay was insistent that the perfect conditions for practice already exist in this present moment. Thus, our practice as Buddhists is to purify our minds so that we can witness the perfection of daily life.

This lesson was epitomized by a teaching I received from Rev. Koyo Kubose, Gyomay Sensei's son and Dharma heir during my training as a Buddhist Lay Minister. For seven days, my fellow trainees and I were expected to place our hands in gassho and give thanks each morning when we used the toilet. This simple gesture forced us to practice mindfulness as we "handled our business."

As a result, using the restroom shifted from something that I did mindlessly into deep spiritual practice. Each time I placed my hands in gassho, I paid attention to my body, mind, feelings, and mental objects. As a result, I noticed how much better I felt after my bowels had been emptied. I reveled in the luxury of indoor plumbing that removed unsightly waste from my life. And I recognized the myriad beings (plumbers, carpenters, wastewater engineers, etc.) who made that moment possible.

In short, using the toilet mindfully showed me how blessed I was each time I engaged in this simple act. It also helped me appreciate the kindness that was being shown to me by other people, which put me in a mindset to be kind to others.

Rev. Koyo often refers to this teaching as "Toilet Gassho"; however, it can be applied to anything. Whether we're walking the dog, washing dishes, or driving the kids to soccer practice, if we approach daily actions with mindfulness, they'll teach us the Buddha Dharma.

**Lesson:** Mindfulness turns every moment into an opportunity for awakening

# Right Concentration

# Lessons from an Outdoor Meditation Retreat

When I was working as an organic farmer/ sustainable builder, I learned to be very self-contained in terms of my Buddhist practice. I had no choice. Farms by their nature are always in the middle of nowhere, and even getting access to online Dharma talks was difficult at times.

As a result, I got used to doing self-led retreats either by myself or with a couple of friends. I also learned how to meditate in some very "strange" places like bus terminals, horse stalls, corn fields, etc. I called upon this experience recently over Memorial Day weekend when I decided to do a two-day, self-led retreat.

The practice was simple. I found a shady spot outside, practiced seated meditation for 45 minutes, and then walked around until I found a new place to sit. Over those two days, I learned some things that will stay with me until my dying day. They are as follows:

## BIRD POOP IS PART OF THE PROCESS

One of the places I chose for my meditation was a park near my house. It was an ideal setting with big leafy trees, park benches, and every bird imaginable singing their hearts out. I put down my cushion on a hillside under one of the larger trees, sat down underneath it, and brought my focus to my breath.

Then the thoughts started. I worried about getting grass stains on my robes. I worried that birds were going to poop on me. I worried that one of the kids skateboarding in the park would have a freak accident and their board would somehow hit me in the head!

But it was too late to worry about any of that. I was committed, and like the Buddha, I was going to sit under that tree until I realized enlightenment, or my meditation timer went off, whichever came first.

As I continued to sit, I realized that my fears were completely unfounded. I wanted to sit in a beautiful park with birds singing in the trees. But you can't enjoy those things without dealing with grass stains and bird poop. They're part of the process and expecting anything else is a cause of suffering.

As humans, we have a lot of strange expectations that cause suffering. We want to earn a paycheck, but we don't want to go to work. We want to drive cars, but we don't want to get stuck in traffic. In other words, we want the good, but we don't want the not-so-good in life, and we suffer as a result.

Thankfully, I didn't get pooped on during my meditation, and I opened my eyes to reasonably clean robes. Thankful for this lesson on acceptance, I packed up my things and walked to the next park.

## WE CAUSE HARM WHEN WE DON'T PAY ATTENTION

During my walk, I practiced mindfulness of the body to maintain my awareness. I focused on the feeling of my feet meeting the pavement with each step, noting the varying amounts of pressure on the ball and heel of each foot as I moved forward.

Finally, I arrived at my designated spot, and I looked around for a suitable place to sit. I found a tree that had no birds in its branches, and I threw my cushion down underneath it in preparation for my practice. Then I sat down, straightened my back, and began to breathe mindfully.

After a short time, I felt the unmistakable tingle of insects crawling on my hands. As every outdoor meditator knows part of the fun is playing the "what's crawling on me now" game.

Flies land on you, ants crawl on you, and the occasional spider attempts to build a web if you hang out for too long. But more often than not the creepy crawlies will be on their way in no time if one sits quietly. So, I refocused my breathing and waited patiently. Only, the creepy crawlies didn't go away. Instead, they were joined by other creepy crawlies! Eventually, I felt one especially brave soul crawl up my arm and then my neck until he was just under my ear.

"Nope!" I thought to myself as I stood up from under the tree. Having insects crawl on me was one thing, but I drew the line at having them crawl in my ear.

As I looked down at my robes, I noticed that my arms were covered in tiny ants. Being careful not to hurt them, I knelt and brushed them off. I watched as they fell to the ground and scurried away. "Where did they all come from," I wondered as I got down on my hands and knees for a closer look. My confusion quickly turned to horror as I realized that I'd been sitting right next to an ant hill. If I had put my cushion down one inch farther to the right, I would've destroyed their home.

Thankfully, I noticed that while my insect friends were agitated with the clumsy human in their midst, they seemed to be largely OK. "Sorry, guys," I whispered as I grabbed my stuff and stepped carefully away from the tree.

As I walked away from the park, I pondered what'd just happened. I didn't pay attention to what was right in front of me, and I nearly killed hundreds of sentient beings as a result. It suddenly made sense why Right Mindfulness is part of the Noble Eightfold Path. Being focused on the present moment is key if we want to ensure our actions benefit everyone around us.

## THE WHOLE WORLD IS MY SANGHA

Next, I decided to meditate next to a lake. It was getting late in the day, and the sun was slowly inching toward the horizon as I took in my surroundings. There were numerous people walking around, and a group of children was screaming gleefully as they chased each other on the grass. I chose a spot under a tree near the shore and sat down on the cushion. There were two women seated nearby; taking selfies. And the lake was filled with people on jet skis and motorboats.

I took a moment to check above me and below me. There were no birds in the branches above me, so I was in little danger of getting pooped on. And there were no tiny insects making their home under the base of the tree, at least none that I could see. Satisfied, I closed my eyes and began the meditation.

As I sat there, the sounds of the world around me filled my ears. My first instinct was to try and block them out, but I learned long ago that this is a losing game. The world will always be there, banging at the front door. The best way to deal with it is by letting it in.

So, I did. I listened to the sounds of jet skis as they ripped past me in the water. I reveled in the sound of leaves rustling in the trees, and chuckled inwardly as the selfie-taking women negotiated who would hold the camera for the next picture.

But as I continued in the meditation, my focus expanded until I heard sounds without attaching any thoughts to them. The sound of leaves rustling above me slowly shifted to become "rustling" and finally just "..."

The boundary between myself and the outside world slowly disintegrated until there was no "me" sitting on the cushion. There was just sound and the raw experience of life exactly as it is. The overall experience was one of deep satisfaction and resounding peace.

Of course, the feeling didn't last forever. Eventually, the timer on my phone went off, and I was pulled back into my body. When I opened my eyes, the women were gone, there were fewer jet skis on the water, and I was alone in the park except for a few stragglers who were watching the sunset.

I started to pack up my things, but I stopped for a moment to reflect on what I'd just experienced. I knew that it was special, and I knew that I should forget about it as quickly as I could. After all, getting attached to special mind-states is a recipe for disaster.

However, I couldn't help but feel like I'd received a gift, or a lesson at the very least. I was able to drop into the deepest meditation when I completely surrendered to everything that was going on around me. I opened myself up to the world, and it responded by helping me in my practice.

The more I thought about it, the more I realized that this had been happening all day. The birds, the ants, and the people at the park had all been supporting me like a traditional Buddhist sangha. They'd taught me lessons and given me exactly what I needed to find my inner stillness.

When we open our eyes and look at the world around us, it becomes clear that we're being supported in several ways. Everyone and everything on the planet is working hard to help us in our walk toward awakening. We just need to open our eyes and notice the gifts that we're given.

A feeling of gratitude filled my heart as I picked up my backpack and put my arms through the straps. It was getting dark, so I'd have to do the next few sitting periods at my apartment. Dutifully, I took a deep breath and began the long walk home.

Lesson- When we walk the Buddhist path, the whole world walks with us.

# The Buddhist Secret to Effective Meditation

Attack the hill is a catchphrase that's heard at least twice during every group bike ride. It's usually shouted at the bottom of elevation changes as a way to motivate cyclists. People tend to slow down when they start climbing a hill. It's an instinctive attempt to avoid the tight muscles and extreme exertion that comes with a hard climb.

The phrase *attack the hill* is meant to shake us out of that mindset, and remind us of what we really need to do to reach the top, pedal harder. This is necessary because as the bike begins to climb, gravity takes over, and we lose forward momentum. In fact, if we give in to the initial instinct to slow down, we may lose all momentum and come to a complete stop. That's why we must pedal hard, with everything we've got in the beginning.

Once that's completed, the name of the game is to keep pedaling. It sounds simple, but when our quads start to burn, and shortness of breath kicks in, it's very tempting to coast for a minute. But the momentary relaxation that comes with coasting results in the loss of forward momentum, momentum that we have to work twice as hard to get back.

Finally, it's important to keep the bike in the highest gear possible. The rookie move is to shift to a low gear so that pedaling will be easier. That's okay for beginners, but all of that easy pedaling results in very slow-going. The more efficient route is to pedal slower, in a much higher gear. It's harder, but it results in more forward motion with each revolution of the pedals. It's also a better workout.

To recap, if we want to ride up a hill in a reasonable amount of time, we need to do three things:

- Attack the hill, and pedal hard in the beginning
- Keep pedaling until we reach the top
- Use the highest gear possible

This method is both simple and effective, but most people don't use it. It's hard, and people don't like doing hard things. So, we shift to a low gear or pick a path with no hills when we ride. Maybe we even go so far as not to ride at all because staying where we're at physically/emotionally is easier than dealing with sore legs and a sweaty body.

Meditation works in much the same way. There's a lot of mysticism and expectation built up around the practice of seated meditation. We hear words like enlightenment and satori, and we think there must be a secret to being a good meditator. In truth, the method for this practice is quite simple.

- Sit on the floor or a cushion in a cross-legged position
- Place your hands in your lap with the palms upward, right hand resting atop the left, and thumbs tips lightly pressed together
- Adopt a noble posture with the spine straight
- Breathe from the stomach, and focus on the feeling of air moving in and out of your lungs
- When your mind wanders, and it will, bring your focus back to the breath without judgment

- Don't move

That's it. That's everything involved in seated meditation, the practice that Buddha himself used to realize enlightenment. But if it's so simple, why are people so unwilling to do it? Perhaps it's because meditation is a lot like riding a bike uphill. It's simple on the surface, but there's a lot of hard work involved.

For example, to do this practice successfully, we must be willing to sit with whatever unpleasantness comes up. We must experience the anxiety of wondering, "Am I doing it right?" We must endure the ache of sore muscles and stiff backs without moving and feel every bit of emotional hurt that manifests itself.

In short, we must be willing to struggle a little bit to practice meditation just like we must be willing to sweat if we want to make it up a hill.

The only secret, if we want to use that word, is consistency. Just like our legs get stronger each time we jump on a bike; our minds get stronger each time we sit on the cushion. Over time, the practice acts as a sort of exposure therapy for our minds. The more we feel anger without giving in to it, the more we experience mental pain without reacting, the less control our emotions have over us.

Eventually, we start to get bored with our thoughts. The same trigger that used to elicit a level twelve meltdown gets downgraded to a seven, and then a three. As our confidence grows, we start going for longer "rides," and the hills we experience during meditation seem smaller. Eventually, they get overshadowed by the inherent contentment that lives within us. But that can't happen if we don't keep pedaling through the hard parts.

That's why we must attack our cushions in the same way that cyclists attack hills. Even if we only meditate for one minute a day, through consistency and hard work, we can realize enlightenment in this lifetime.

**Lesson:** Attack the cushion!

## Stillness and Storms

In August 2005, Hurricane Katrina crashed into the Gulf of Mexico and caused nearly $100 billion in property damage. As a result of the storm, numerous levees broke in the city of New Orleans, and the ensuing flood left much of the city underwater. In the aftermath, I volunteered to convoy to New Orleans' 9th ward with other members of my Marine unit to help with the relief effort. Sadly, we were only there for a short time before another disaster struck.

Less than a month after Hurricane Katrina hit, we received news that a second hurricane was en route. This one was called Hurricane Rita, and she was Category 5 storm with wind speeds of up to 177 mph. After some deliberation, our command decided that the best thing for us to do would be to ride out the storm at sea. So, we loaded all of our equipment aboard the U.S.S. Shreveport and ventured out into the Gulf of Mexico.

It was at this point that I found out that I get horribly seasick. Of course, I'd been on boats before this. In fact, I earned the sailing merit badge when I was in Boy Scouts.

But there's a big difference between maneuvering a sailboat on a calm lake and living on a Navy ship when it's being tossed about by a hurricane! But I still had a job to do. So, I fell into a steady rhythm of eating, working, and throwing up that sustained me for the length of our voyage. But it wasn't all bad news.

One night I was operating the radios on the bridge when word came down that we were about to enter the eye of the hurricane. This was the experience of a lifetime, and it was pure, dumb luck that I happened to be on duty when it happened. But it's an experience that I'll never forget.

One minute we were rocking violently back and forth in the waves, and the next minute everything was perfectly calm. The sound of ocean water battering the side of the ship ceased, and I could hear our engines humming as we moved steadily through the water. As I looked out the windows, the sky which had been pitch black a moment ago was suddenly filled with stars, and I felt like I could count all of them if given enough time.

I'm not sure how long we were in the eye, but before I knew what was happening, we were back amid the storm. I responded by promptly throwing up.

For many of us, the comings and goings of daily life can feel like a never-ending storm. There's always one more item to check off the to-do list, and one more person we need to check-in with. Have the kids been fed? Are we prepared for tomorrow's meeting? Should we pick up the dry cleaning on Friday or Saturday? If we're not careful, we can run ourselves ragged trying to keep up with it all. But in the end, it all still needs to get done.

During these types of storms, meditation can be our eye of the hurricane. It can provide a place of stillness right there in the middle of our struggles. To a certain degree, it doesn't matter what else is going on in our lives. Because our cushion is always there waiting for us. And as the Buddha sits patiently on our altar, we can choose to sit for a spell, close our eyes, and revel in the stillness of our minds.

Of course, when we finish our meditation, the storm will still be waiting for us. But our minds will be prepared to deal with it.

**Lesson:** Meditation makes us the eye of the storm

## Complicated Watches

My fascination with watches started when I was 8 years old. My maternal grandfather had a mechanical gold watch that he cherished, and he let me watch him when he took it apart to make repairs. I couldn't understand how they made the pieces so small or how he always remembered what part went where, but he did.

And I spent many afternoons chatting with him as he sat hunched over his workbench. Unfortunately, I didn't inherit his mechanical aptitude. My watches go straight to the jeweler when they need repairs. But his deep love of timepieces lives firmly in my heart.

Besides nostalgia, my deep respect for mechanical watches comes with their inherent usefulness throughout human history. They were the de facto smartphones of their day, and each one had one or more "complications" that allowed them to keep track of the time, date, and whatever else the watchmaker needed.

Naturally, the more complications they had, the more expensive they became. So much so that in 2014 Sotheby's auctioned off a watch for $24 million that kept track of the time, date, sunrise and sunset, moon phases, and even had a constellation map that told the original owner what constellations he could see from his New York apartment on any given night.[37]

However, those delightful complications come with a price. The tiny gears and springs that make up a mechanical watch generate friction as they grind against each other. Additionally, their movements either speed up or slow down based on the temperature and humidity. So, mechanical watches must be wound regularly. And they don't keep time as accurately as their digital counterparts.

However, mechanical watches possess a certain romance that their digital counterparts will never match. There's beauty in the craftsmanship required to make gears and springs work smoothly within a timepiece. And there's joy in learning the history of a watch that's been in a family for generations. Yes, mechanical watches require more work. But in many ways that extra work is an asset, not a detriment. The same can is true for human life.

Each of us has several complications that we deal with every day (work, family, hobbies, etc.). And the first seven tenets of the Noble Eightfold Path help us decide which ones we should keep and which ones we should throw away. But there comes a point when we can't reasonably let go of anything else, and we need to deal with the messiness of what's left. We have to do this in the same way that a mechanical watch owner must wind her timepiece at the end of each day.

For Buddhists, the practice of Right Concentration is how we "wind" our spiritual clocks in response to the hectic nature of daily life. When we concentrate single-pointedly on an object as part of meditation, we bring ourselves back to center. And we're able to respond correctly to life's troubles in the same way that a clock returns to telling time correctly one it's been reset.

There are many ways to practice single-pointed concentration. However, the way that is most commonly practiced is concentration on the breath. We sit cross-legged on the cushion, straighten our backs, and breathe. Focusing on the feeling of air moving in and out of our lungs and feeling of chest expanding and contracting, we pull ourselves out of the manic thought patterns that bring stress into our lives. When our minds wander, we notice, and gently bring our attention back to our breathing.

Another method for practicing single-pointed concentration is through body scans. Using the same seated posture that was mentioned above, we start by bringing our attention to our feet. And we concentrate on them, noticing the physical sensations therein. Are they sore? Are they sweaty?

After we spend some time on our feet, we bring our attention to our calves being careful not to generate any extraneous thoughts, just noticing physical sensations. If our minds wander, we notice, and bring our concentration back to our body. We continue this exercise until we get to the top of our head.

Ideally, we want to engage in single-pointed concentration at least once daily. The length of time we do it is less important than the consistency. In other words, it's better to practice meditation for one minute every day than to do it for one hour every week. Traditionally, it's done while sitting cross-legged on a cushion. However, the beauty of the practice is that it can be done when we're driving, sitting in a coffee shop, or even when we're getting a root canal from the dentist.

The key thing to remember is that our lives, like a mechanical watch, are imperfect. But it's the imperfection that makes them beautiful. And the practice of single-pointed concentration helps us work skillfully with any complications that may arise.

**Lesson:** Single-pointed concentration makes a complicated life run smoothly.

## Single-Pointed Contentment

When we practice single-pointed concentration, we take our mental focus and bring it to bear on a single object. If our minds wander, then we direct them back to the object, or the task, or the person in front of us. This sounds easy to do in theory, but most people must practice for many years before they can truly focus their attention.

That's because our minds are trained to seek after new and exciting things. If we buy a car, we want a faster one. If our TV show goes to commercial, we check to see what's on the other channel. We never focus on what's in front of us because we're constantly checking to see what else is out there. As a result, we often feel restless and anxious for no reason. It's not that things are bad, per se. We just wonder how they could be better.

Thankfully, the practice of single-pointed concentration helps us to do away with all of that. It teaches us how to be content with what we have in the here and now. However, it's not an easy journey. Most of us have years of mental habits that need to be unlearned before we can stop searching for the next best thing. That's why consistency is so important.

For example, when we engage with the practice through seated meditation; sitting on the cushion and focusing on our breath, our minds will start to wander. We'll think about the bill that needs to be paid, or what we want to have for dinner, or one of a host of other things. So, the practice becomes a cycle of losing and then restoring our concentration. In a way, we must learn to be stubborn. Like a donkey that refuses to pull a cart, we must sit on the cushion and refuse to move from that spot.

Each time we do this, our mind settles a little more, and we're able to maintain our concentration a little longer. Eventually, we stop searching for something better to do, and we learn to be content with focusing on the breath. We may even enjoy it after a while, finding it to be peaceful and refreshing.

Of course, the next step is to take our single-pointed concentration off the cushion. If we can learn to be content with nothing but our breath, then there's no reason we can't be content while washing dishes, or speaking to a loved one, or using the restroom. We just need to be stubborn and teach ourselves to see nothing outside of our concentration object.

When we do this, the entire world opens to us. It does this not because we have everything that we were looking for, but because we've learned to stop looking. This happens in the same way that we learn to stop checking our cell phone during meditation.

Thus, our single-pointed concentration becomes single-pointed contentment. And we learn to be both happy and fulfilled by the countless objects that make up our daily life.

**Lesson:** We already have everything we need.

## Learn More at the Following Websites:

**Blog:** https://thesameoldzen.com

**Twitter:** https://twitter.com/sameoldzen

**Facebook:** https://www.facebook.com/TheSameOldZen/

**YouTube:** http://www.youtube.com/c/SenseiAlexKakuyo

**Instagram:** https://www.instagram.com/alexkakuyo/

# Notes

1. A Basic Buddhism Guide: The Eight-Fold Path, buddhanet.net/e-learning/8foldpath.htm.

2. Andang, Angky. "Greedy Monkey." YouTube, YouTube, 19 Jan. 2017, www.youtube.com/watch?v=qg-XWIo6Gk4.

3. The Group of Discourse (Sutta-Nipata) Translated by K.R. Norman, PaliText Society, 2$^{nd}$ edition, Lancaster, 2008 page 78

4. Culinary Fundamentals Shojin Ryori - Shabkar.Org. www.shabkar.org/download/pdf/Shojin_Ryori_Culinary_Fundamentals_in_Zen.pdf.

5. Post, South China Morning. "Zen Buddhist Nun Jeong Kwan's Korean Temple Food Philosophy." YouTube, YouTube, 2 Nov. 2017, www.youtube.com/watch?v=X3KIDY8JN3U.

6. Từ Thanh. Buddhism for Beginners. M. Trung, 1998.

7. "Freedom." Dictionary.com, Dictionary.com, www.dictionary.com/browse/freedom.

8. Lopez, Donald S. "Four Noble Truths." Encyclopædia Britannica, Encyclopædia Britannica, Inc., 14 Mar. 2017, www.britannica.com/topic/Four-Noble-Truths.

9. Adapted from a teaching that was given by Zhuangzhi in Zhuangzi: The Essential Writings: With Selections from Traditional Commentaries, p. 84-86

10. Internet Archive. "I and Thou." https://archive.org/stream/IAndThou_572/BuberMartin-i-and-thou_djvu.txt

11. "Amongst White Clouds (Zen Documentary)." YouTube, 16 Feb. 2014, youtu.be/vALIr2qJTeU.

12. Kaccayanagotta Sutta (Samyutta Nikaya 12.15)

13. "BibleGateway." 1 Corinthians 12:1-13 KJV - - Bible Gateway, www.biblegateway.com/passage/?search=1 Corinthians 12:1-13&version=KJV.

14. National Geographic Society. "Giant Buddha, Giant Ears." National Geographic Society, 9 Nov. 2012, www.nationalgeographic.org/media/buddha-ears/.The Birth of the Buddha. I. The Buddha. Translated from the Introduction to the Jtaka (i. 4721). 1909-14. Buddhist Writings. The Harvard Classics, www.bartleby.com/45/3/102.html.

15. Ahmann, Mathew H., and Stephen J. Wright. *The New Negro.: James Baldwin*. 1965.

16. Buddhaghosa, and Ñāṇamoli . *The Path of Purification: (Visuddhimagga)*. Shambhala, 1976.

17. O'Brien, Barbara. "What Does Buddhism Teach About Right Speech?" *Learn Religions*, Learn Religions, 21 Jan. 2019, https://www.learnreligions.com/right-speech-450072.

18. O'Brien, Barbara. "What Does Buddhism Teach About Right Speech?" *Learn Religions*, Learn Religions, 21 Jan. 2019, https://www.learnreligions.com/right-speech-450072.

19. Petersen, James C. Why Don't We Listen Better?: Communicating & Connecting in Relationships. BookBaby, 2007.

20. Prasoon, Shrikant. Knowing Buddha. Hindoology Books, 2007.
21. Buddhist Studies: Number of Buddhist World-Wide, www.buddhanet.net/e-learning/history/bud_statwrld.htm.
22. "Liturgy." Dictionary.com, Dictionary.com, www.dictionary.com/browse/liturgy.
23. "Formulary." Dictionary.com, Dictionary.com, www.dictionary.com/browse/formulary.

24. Vonnegut, Kurt. *Mother Night*. New York: Delta Trade Paperbacks, 1999. Print.

25. "FEATURES: COLUMNS: Theravada Teachings." *Buddhistdoor*, https://www.buddhistdoor.net/features/concerning-right-action-and-right-livelihood.
26. "Confucianism and Buddhism." *Encyclopedia of Buddhism*, Encyclopedia.com, 24 Dec. 2019, https://www.encyclopedia.com/religion/encyclopedias-almanacs-transcripts-and-maps/confucianism-and-buddhism.
27. https://anchor.fm/around-grandfather-fire/episodes/AGF-15---KARMA--with-Sensei-Alex-e38ld9
28. Besserman, Perle, and Manfred Steger. *Crazy Clouds: Zen Radicals, Rebels, and Reformers*. Shambhala, 1991.
29. "The Five Hindrances." *One Mind Dharma*, 21 Mar. 2019, https://oneminddharma.com/five-hindrances/.
30. Chikako Ozawa-de Silva (2007). Demystifying Japanese Therapy: An Analysis of Naikan and the

Ajase Complex through Buddhist Thought, Ethos 35, (4), 411–446

31. My memory is a bit fuzzy, but these are the prices as best as I can remember them

32. Ono Yōko, and John Lennon. Grapefruit: A Book of Instructions Drawings. Simon & Schuster, 2007.

33. "About the Garden." Lansu Chinese Garden, lansugarden.org/about-the-garden

34. Christakis, Holly B. ShakyaNicholas A. "A New, More Rigorous Study Confirms: The More You Use Facebook, the Worse You Feel." Harvard Business Review, 21 Aug. 2017, hbr.org/2017/04/a-new-more-rigorous-study-confirms-the-more-you-use-facebook-the-worse-you-feel.

35. Pandita, Sayadaw U, et al. "What Is Vipassana Meditation and How Do You Practice It?" Lion's Roar, 3 Dec. 2018, www.lionsroar.com/how-to-practice-vipassana-insight-meditation/.

36. http://www.buddhanet.net/pdf_file/pureland.pdf

37. "World's Most Expensive Watch Sold at Auction." BBC News, BBC, 12 Nov. 2014, www.bbc.com/ncws/av/world-europe-30015601/world-s-most-cxpensive-watch-sold-at-auction.

Made in the USA
Monee, IL
12 October 2021

79882288R00142